EXCELLENCE IN MANAGEMENT

TOTAL QUALITY

EXCELLENT ORGANIZATIONS, SUCCESSFUL ORGANIZATIONS

Updated September 2016

Enrique Miguel Sánchez Motos

esm@adlc.es

Front and back cover developed by Miguel Angel Segura Ureta based on an image of www.freepik.es

To Marcia, my excellent wife

INDEX

1 INTRODUCTION

2 WHAT DOES SUCCESS MEAN?

3 THE MANAGER AND THE ORGANIZATION'S MISSION

4 PLANNING: GREAT ALLY AND TERRIBLE ENEMY
4.1 STRATEGIC PLANNING
4.2 MANAGEMENT BY OBJECTIVES
4.3 RISKS OF THE STRATEGIC PLANNING AND MBO

5 ORGANIZATIONAL STRUCTURE

6 THE DIRECTOR AS STAFF MANAGER
6.1 MANAGER'S NATURAL QUALITIES
6.2 MANAGER'S ACQUIRED ABILITIES
6.3 ORGANIZATION CHARACTERISTICS
6.4 STAFF'S INTERESTS AND MOTIVATION
6.5 MAIN STAFF MOTIVATION THEORIES

7 AFTER THEORY COMES PRACTICE

8 THE QUALITY CONCEPT

8.1 A CONCEPT OFTEN MISUNDERSTOOD
8.2 PRODUCT QUALITY
    8.2.1 Quality from the client's point of vie
    8.2.2 Quality from the point of view of the company
    8.2.3 Simultaneous quality for the customer and the organization
8.3 PROCESS QUALITY
8.4 TOTAL QUALITY MANAGEMENT
    8.4.1 What Total Quality is
    8.4.2 What Total Quality is not
    8.4.3 Definitions of Total Quality Management

9 THE FOUR PILLARS

9.1 EXTERNAL CLIENTS
9.2 INTERNAL CLIENTS
    9.2.1 Disparity between Managers and Employees' opinions
    9.2.2 Providers as Internal Clients
9.3 PROCESSES
9.4 CONTINUOUS IMPROVEMENT

10 BENCHMARKING

10.1 WHAT CHARACTERISTICS CAN BE COMPARED?
10.2 HOW TO COLLECT THE ADEQUATE INFORMATION
10.3 BENCHMARKING DATA COLLECTION RECOMMENDATIONS
10.4 IN WHAT MOMENT IS IT GOOD TO MAKE COMPARISONS?

10.5 BENCHMARKING LIMITS

11 QUALITY COSTS

11.1 FUNCTIONING COSTS AND QUALITY COSTS
11.2 NON-QUALITY COSTS
11.3 HOW WILL NON-QUALITY COSTS BE CALCULATED?

12 QUALITY CIRCLES OR IMPROVEMENT GROUPS

12.1 WHAT ARE QUALITY CIRCLES?
12.2 PHILOSOPHY OF QUALITY CIRCLES
12.3 HOW TO MOTIVATE QUALITY CIRCLES
12.4 QC PERFORMANCE EVALUATION
12.5 REQUIREMENTS FOR THE QC SUCCESS

13 THE ORGANIZATIONAL STRUCTURE FOR THE EXCELLENCE

14 HOW TO IMPLEMENT EXCELLENCE

15 IMPLEMENTING EXCELLENCE: MOST FREQUENT MISTAKES

16 ASSESSING WHETHER EXCELLENCE IS REALLY BEING APPLIED

16.1 THE EFQM MODEL. ITS ORIGIN
16.2 EFQM MODEL CONTENTS
    16.2.1 The EFQM nine criteria
    16.1.2 The PDCA circle
    16.1.3 EFQM scoring system

17 CONCLUSIONS

18 BIBLIOGRAPHIES

SECTION I.

THE ORGANIZATION AND SUCCESS

1 INTRODUCTION

In management, the main challenge is to **lead** the organization towards success and to **keep** it there. Opportunistic success, the success of a moment, the success derived from a fortuitous decision, or the success of an investment realized by chance is mere appearance and vanishes soon. It is just chance, not success.

We must differentiate the success that comes as the result of the manager's performance from the "success" of those who, by chance, win the first prize in the lottery.

Success, when it is due to the action of a manager, is a relatively stable situation that allows the organization **to achieve good results steadily,** within the framework of its mission or rationale and despite the changes in the socio-economic context. Obviously, excluding the impact produced by natural disasters or major social or economic unexpected crises.

Success, as the result of a manager's performance, **requires knowhow**, medium or long-term **vision** and a **management philosophy**.

The improvisation -used in the past when leading organizations- and the self-oriented leadership style have given way to the search of forms of management whose logic and rationality allow a conscious management of the available resources of the organization.

Consequently, the use of any management style became not just the outcome of a leader's fortuitous inspiration but the result of a deep understanding of the different topics a manager should take into account.

There is not only one way of management, one only absolute standard, one valid prescription for all times and circumstances. Instead, what managers have found out is a variety of managerial answers on how to optimize the use of the organizational resources, and achieve the desired results.

These answers vary over time. Today an author may emphasize some management aspects. Tomorrow, different authors will suggest emphasizing other aspects.

Fred Taylor[1] stressed the importance of focusing on the review of the production **processes**. Others, such as Münsterberg[2],

---

[1] Frederick Wilson Taylor (1856-1917), author of the "Scientific Organization of Work." His most famous and important book was the "Principles of Scientific Management" published in 1911.

[2] Hugo Münsterberg (1836-1916), considered the father of Industrial Psychology. His best-known book is "Psychology and Efficiency in Industry", published in 1912.

emphasized the importance of the manager as a **good psychologist** to motivate the employees and create a suitable environment. Others, like Elton Mayo[3], stressed that the most important thing is to create a good human relations environment within the company, etc.

Subsequently, the question became even more complex.

It was observed that it was not enough to focus on the optimization of the various factors that were involved in the production process. It was not enough to worry about technology, or about the design of the processes, or the psychological management of human resources, or the creation of a climate of good human relations within the organization.

It was also necessary to take into account many other factors such as:
- The increasing variability of the social economic environment
- The businesses expectations
- The type of products and services required
- The changes in technology
- The market expansion

---

[3] George Elton Mayo (1880-1949), considered the founder of industrial sociology and especially of the "Theory of Human Relations." He published in 1933 "The Human Problems of Industrial Civilization"

- The emergence of new competitors
- The new political and social contexts
- The need to find an inner balance between power, responsibility and functional autonomy
- Etc.

The plurality of factors having impact on the success of an organization led to the conclusion that **there was no magic recipe** for management. Nor was it possible to leave success to the providential emergence of a charismatic leader with quasi-miraculous powers, possessing a crystal ball to see the future and propose actions.

Then, a growing interest in the study of the managerial function arose related to the aspects of management, organization, control and coordination. This was reflected in a significant expansion of the so-called Business Schools.

They defended the idea that the role of the manager is a **profession** based on a deep knowledge of principles, methodologies and specific management techniques.

Numerous works have been published and issued because of that interest. Some are general study manuals; some others address specific aspects (leadership, strategy, planning, teams, etc); others present concrete experiences of management and others propose a specific philosophy and a particular management practice.

This book falls into the latter group and advocates for the use of **Excellence**, originally known as Total Quality Management (TQM).
The change of the name of this management philosophy **from TQM to Excellence** is geared to emphasize the fact that its proposals are not the same as those of the so-called "quality systems", which are centered on certifying "Quality Processes" systems (such as ISO 9000 and similar models), but on a comprehensive and **holistic approach** to the Management role.

Excellence considers that an excellent management combines a comprehensive management of all **organization's resources** (including the leadership style, the human resources, the material and technological resources and the processes) and has at the same time **a global focus on results** (economic, clients satisfaction, human resources satisfaction and society impact).

A lot of books write about Quality. But indeed, what is Quality Management?

In the 8th European Quality Conference (Luxembourg, October 2015), Professor Y. Emery from the University of Lausanne Switzerland, pointed out **three key ideas:**

1. Quality Management has become highly technical and is frequently associated with every kind of label and certification: **the very origins of QM have been forgotten.**

2. Amazing amount of organizations, publications, specialized journals, norms and quality frameworks, consultants and prizes: **but what is quality?**

3. Quality Management tends to be perceived as dehumanized and is **frequently criticized** by professionals who feel not recognized: **is there a way to reconcile** Managers, QM specialists and professionals?

This book is very much in line with Prof. Y Emery`s ideas.

It underlines that the original Quality Management, later known as Total Quality Management (TQM) and, nowadays Excellence, is risking to be hidden behind the trees (methodologies, labels, certifications, etc). *"The forest cannot be seen for the trees"*

That is the reason why this book begins by making a brief approach to the main management topics such as leadership, strategy and planning, management by objectives and human resources management.

In fact, Excellence or Total Quality Management takes a clear position regarding all these management issues.

Therefore, this book aims at people of action and high level managers, who are often overwhelmed by the intense daily work.

Aware that time is money, or at least a scarce resource, this book has attempted to use a clear, direct language, likely to reveal, with an easily understandable terminology, the essential factors that can transform or consolidate a normal organization into a successful one.

In addition, specific measures, considered as the most appropriate to streamline the organization and lead it to success, are explained, justified and submitted to the reader's consideration.

This book also aims at **teachers and students** of Management Techniques. The theoretical truth illuminates the practical experience, and that allows, in turn, internalizing the theoretical truth.

Teachers and students can contrast Excellence with the general theoretical framework on management and analyze its advantages and disadvantages in comparison to other existing proposals.

Every manager should be aware of the management **philosophy** he uses since **it will impregnate his behavior.** All specific techniques, such as Strategic Planning, Management by Objectives (MBO), Evaluation of Merit, Work Teams, Organization by Processes, etc. will work very differently according to the top manager's philosophical framework.

The word "philosophy" should not lead us to think that this book is a theoretical book. Rather the opposite: **it is a practical book**, which begins by posing a global issue: **"what is success?"**

Then, **it reflects on the main elements** on which the management function resides.

Next, **it proposes a clear philosophy** accompanied of a framework of concrete management lines that are essential for the successful management of an organization.

The book concludes by **presenting, as a concrete example, a specific excellence model**, the European Business Excellence Model, deeply connected with the Japanese and American ones. **All of them are very valuable** for managers in order to check -through self-assessment- **if they are properly applying** the key necessary pillars of an Excellent Management.

We will be available for any review or comments at the email: esm@adlc.es

2 WHAT DOES SUCCESS MEAN?

The aim of any professional manager is that his organization becomes successful.

However, what is success? There are many answers to this question.

For a precious stone seeker, success means to find a valuable emerald.

For a gambler, success means to win an important lottery prize.

For a businessperson, success could mean the generation of high profit by taking advantage of a situation of shortage to export his products at much higher prices than the usual on the market.

For other business people, success may be the creation of a product that will be more widely accepted by the consumers, etc.

Therefore, there are **many different views** in regards to what we understand by success.

However, none of these given examples fit in with the definition of success proposed in this book, because none of them guarantees the continuation of the state of being successful after the lucky moments are gone.

We will suggest the following definition:

Success at a mission means **to obtain, steadily, the results that were once set up as**

objectives and to gain through them **a high net added value** (benefit).

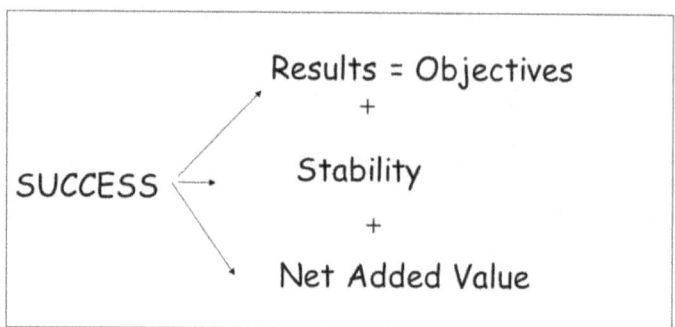

Therefore, the success we are talking about is not unforeseen; it is rather a success that is **achieved** when the results obtained **fit in with the previously defined objectives**.

The idea that the results must fit in with the objectives requires a **previous** definition of the **objectives** and a **later** activity in order to obtain the results sought as objectives. It excludes any "success" obtained by chance. It means achieving **"success" at the mission** we are working on.

The definition of success also involves two elements: **stability** and **value**, whose meanings need definition.

We understand by **stability** the ability to maintain a certain situation in time. In our case, the success of an organization requires maintaining in time the adequacy between results and objectives.

Considering the fact that **reality is continuously changing** (*"nobody swims twice in the water of the same river"*, said Heraclitus[4]), the objectives must evolve and therefore the results must fit in with the new definition of objectives.

Nevertheless, the big organization objectives only vary radically if the mission of the organization changes substantially.

Therefore, it is reasonable to expect a certain stability of the objectives. That does not exclude the fact that an evolution of both the products and the processes could happen and, therefore, a change of the internal (processes, organizational structure, etc) as well as of the external relations (clients, products, etc) of the organization.

For example, there is no doubt that Ford is considered to be a successful company because it has maintained certain stability between its objectives (obtaining success in the car manufacturing activity) and its business results. Even so, products and manufacturing forms, manager-employees and firm-clients relations have gone through a radical evolution in the last 50 years.

---

[4] Heráclitus (535.435 a.C.) Greek philosopher of the Miletus School, in Asia Minor

The definition of success that we have proposed includes the concept of *"obtaining a **high added value**"*. What should we understand by this?

The **concept of value** refers not only to the economic result obtained through the activities carried out by the organization, but also to the improvement of the market value that an organization well managed can obtain through its position, image, creativity, management culture, labor relations culture, vision of the future, etc.

The idea of **added value (benefit)** refers to the actual value of the organization compared to its value at a previous moment. This added value has been the addition of value generated by the activities of the organization, plus the increase of the value of the organization itself (its market or social value).

The concept of **net added value** refers to the products generated value, minus the cost to produce the products value. It also refers to the value of the organization subtracting the costs involved in the increase of the value of the organization (training, expansion to new markets, image, intellectual properties, investments, etc)

The net added value **refers to** the surplus or **differential** represented by the value of its **reached** position **in comparison** to the position at

departure, minus the used means to generate the new level of value.

The net value may also be defined, for a certain period, as the addition of the net **profits** and growths of the organization's **value**. This net **added value can be negative** when instead of profits there are losses or when the market or social value of the organization diminishes.

The concept of profit, depending on the type of organization, refers to the economic profit of the companies operating on the market, but it may also refer to other types of profit, as, for example, the good image that a hospital may have in a city.

The growth of the organization value concerns the differential value between the newly reached situation and the point at departure. Thus, for example, in the case of the companies operating on the market, if the company is listed on the Stock Exchange, a reference has to be made to the growth of the organization value compared to the initial value of its shares.

This growth in value may exceed greatly the annual profits derived from the production and sales processes. The growth in value can be higher than the amount that we would obtain by capitalizing the profits of that company or organization.

On the Stock Exchange market it is very common to find that the amount which represents the value of the shares of a company is much larger that the amount that could be obtained by capitalizing, in the long term, the profits that the company obtained in the last financial year. This is because the Stock Exchange not only considers the economic performance of the company, but also the expectations of future benefits foreseen due to creativity, stability, influence, structure and dynamism of each company.

The idea of success is not only limited to the companies which operate on the market. There are many organizations whose success is not measured by economic results.

For example, the success of a political party can be measured through its electoral results (number of votes, evolution of the voting intentions compared to the previous situation) and by the improvement of **its global value** as an organization (its consolidation as a Party or the increase of its political possibilities to reach the government office in the next elections).

In the case of a particular Government, **its value** may refer to its capacity to accomplish its objectives: the expansion of the employment rate, the implementation of the national education system, the decreasing delinquency rate, the improvement of its transparency and trustworthy or reliable image, the reduction of the public deficit, etc.

3 THE MANAGER AND THE ORGANIZATION'S MISSION

The management role is decisive to achieve success.

The mission is the "why" of the organization's existence. The management must **develop** the organization's mission. It is also his duty to reflect and, if the case may be, redesign the mission.

The first challenge that the management has to undertake is the adoption of a **solid position**, from a conceptual point of view, **in full accordance with the mission** or the general goal of the organization.

This position includes the option to dissolve the organization, if the management[5] estimates that the organization is not viable. In military terms, when winning a war is impossible or farfetched, to surrender may be contemplated as a way to relieve society of bigger problems.

In the dialectics between Mission and Means, **the mission comes first; the means come afterwards**. This does not mean that it is appropriate to design fantastic or even impossible

---

[5] Let's recall that there are managers specialized in liquidating and recycling companies

missions, without considering whether the necessary means to accomplish them are available.

Establishing **the mission** and its contents is the **first step** to take; **then**, before putting it into practice, it has to go through **the filter of the availability of means** that would be needed or that could be obtained.

Anyway, **the first and most important thing is to have a clear idea** where the organization wants to arrive at.

After defining the global and the concrete objectives, it is time to see and make sure that we have the necessary means (methodology, tools and resources).

If we do not have them or we cannot obtain them, we should redefine the objectives, in the mission's framework, in order to establish a new level of objectives adequate to the available means. It might even be necessary to propose a radical change of the mission if the available means do not fit in with the mission.

The mission of the organization must be ambitious, but not impossible. In many cases, the impossibility to attain the mission is due to real circumstances and to the fact that the availability of the means are not taken into account, leading the organization to failure.

One of the greatest difficulties that the strategists face is to analyze and assess accurately the context in which the mission is supposed to be developed.

Napoleon and Hitler fought against the climate and the huge surfaces of Russia.

The roughness of the Russian winter and the long distances largely contributed to their respective military failures.

Similarly, the search of El Dorado by Lope de Aguirre was struck by the unreality of the myth: we cannot find something that does not exist.

The American government failed in Vietnam when the media changed the public opinion, defending an unconditional withdrawal.

All these examples underline the fact that to be successful it is fundamental to be aware of the reality in which the mission is going to be developed.

In a previous chapter, we referred to **Heraclitus**. This Greek philosopher said that everything is in continuous change. The water of a river flows constantly and that is why he said that we could never bathe twice in the same water. Heraclitus' sentence was *"**we can never bathe twice** in the water of the same river"*.

Nevertheless, another Greek philosopher, **Parmenides**[6], in opposition to Heraclitus, pointed out the opposite: *"nothing is changing in reality because the essence is immutable"*. He was also right. Even if we do not bathe in the same water, the river remains the same and therefore we may say that we bathe in the same river.

Similarly, every manager should always remember: he must have **a concept of the essence of the value he is looking for.** Then, he should set the objectives defined to get this type of value, and later analyze the results in order to assess if the searched values have been really achieved through those results.

If what he considers today as the essence of value -for example, the yearly economic profit- changes suddenly into another value, such as the company image or market expansion, then he will never be able to establish clear objectives. There should be some permanent value. Otherwise, the management may fall into leading an organization without direction or clear goals, as a chicken with its head off.

A leader can set up economic success as his general goal.

However, he should be ready to face the total transformation of his company, even

---

[6] Parmenides (539 – 480 b.C.) Greek philosopher of the Elea school, in a Greek colony in the South of Italy

abandoning the previous production range, if it has become obsolete, and start a different production line. Nevertheless, he should be always seeking to achieve the same global goal: economic profit (or whatever else).

The value he is seeking to achieve is essential and permanent and, on a secondary place, is the type of the organization's activity, which is modifiable.

The objectives **are a key point to achieve success. Nevertheless,** it would be inadequate to define objectives and to persevere, year after year and at all costs, until these objectives are reached.

It is **necessary to review the objectives periodically** in order to ensure their feasibility and adaptability to the changing conditions of the environment.

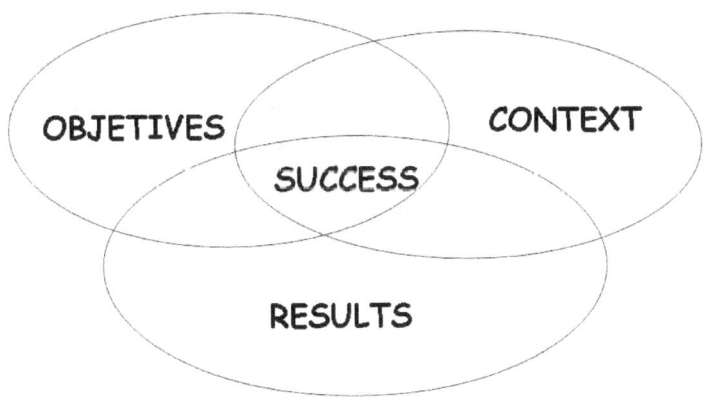

Objectives, Results and Environment are the three sides of the triangle of success.

The manager has the direct responsibility over the first two.

Nevertheless, the Environment escapes, in great measure, to his control. It may vary according to political circumstances, social situation, international markets, etc.

The manager, regarding the Environment, has the responsibility to be reasonably informed about forecasts, expectations and innovations. It is logical that the manager dedicates **part of his time** analyzing the information regarding the general **perspectives** of the local, national and global economic and social evolution that can affect the functioning of the organization.

A phrase worth considering is the following: *"The leaders adapt to the changes. They provoke them and take the initiative".*

It highlights the responsibility of the manager to be attentive to the changes of the economic or social environment, to react wisely to them, to foresee them and even to provoke them, if necessary, in order to take the initiative.

4 PLANNING: GREAT ALLY AND TERRIBLE ENEMY

Deliberation, decision making and good management do not guarantee success by themselves.

Success is sure only when you reach it. However, to keep the same level of success, certain managing actions, such as planning, are necessary efforts in order to obtain good and steady results: that is, success.

Planning is the process of thinking which helps the manager to adopt decisions towards short, medium and long-term future.

It is a very efficient management method but, just by itself, it cannot guarantee success. For example, in the military field, when two armies are fighting, each has its respective strategic plan but only one will win the war.

Fortunately, the field of economy and social life is not like a military scenario, in which the victory is always obtained by defeating the enemy. Economic and social life allows for the growth of the profit of all parties, without the need of exterminating the competitor or opponent.

The history of the nations shows pretty clearly that the wealth and wellbeing of all people can increase. If all the nations were listed on a hypothetical Stock Exchange, we would notice that their global value today would be superior to that of 10, 20 or 50 years ago.

Indeed, with few exceptions in the world, the Gross Domestic Product and the national income per capita have increased, not only in nominal terms, but also in real terms (after the deduction of the effect of inflation).

This proves that the global wealth is not a limited cake of which what somebody wins is due to somebody else's loss. Therefore, the main challenge of any manager is to be ready to manage efficiently, even creating new production lines, in order to generate value.

Besides that, managers should be ready to give up those products or services that are not in demand anymore. **The reorientation of the use of available resources is a crucial management responsibility**.

The following sentence *"when there is a need on the market everybody hears about it, but only a leader listens to it"* greatly reflects reality. Not every manager behaves as an innovator leader; many just follow the ways opened by others. To be able to respond to the market or society needs, the manager should have **Vision**.

Planning is one of the instruments that **must help the leader to scrutinize the horizon**, to have a flair for the business. I am pointing out that **planning "must be a help" instead of an obstacle**, as it sometimes is.

This happens when the plan is elaborated far from reality or when it is so rigid that it slows and makes it difficult to take any decisions or to quickly adapt to new circumstances.

When this happens, the diagnosis is clear: the leader was not able to create an efficient planning mechanism and should proceed to restructure it urgently.

Another important purpose of the planning is **to facilitate the organization's adaptation to changes**.

Reacting to unexpected situations should be avoided at all times as much as possible. Different unforeseen circumstances may always appear, but the organizations should have reflected sufficiently and beforehand about the possible directions of the changes, in order to be in the position to even cause the change and take the initiative.

Planning must also be an instrument that **confirms how suitable the means to reach the objectives of the organization are**. By breaking down the bigger objectives into more concrete and specific ones, it becomes easier to work out the necessary means that will be needed to achieve each of the objectives, and therefore, to estimate the adequacy of those means that are available.

4.1 Strategic Planning

The strategic planning is the most dynamic and complicated type of planning. The word "strategy" refers to a **rational choice** of the main action lines, after other possible action lines have been assessed carefully.

This general enumeration of possible strategic lines can be made after considering:
- **Strengths** or main capacities of the organization
- **Weaknesses** or lacks
- **Opportunities** for action offered by the environment and
- **Threats** which come from the environment and that need to be dealt with, such as the market crisis, the pressure by the competitors or the effect of other negative circumstances.

The manager, with the help and suggestions of his co-workers, must establish the strategic planning.

The range and **diversity of points of view** between the individual who chooses risk and the one who proposes well-known ways; between the one who thinks and the one who executes; between the one who focuses on the economic results and the one who underlines social aspects, etc, is an **unlimited source of ideas for** the management.

The strategic planning established by a manager who prefers his collaborators to say *"yes, sir"* to all his decisions is the worst strategic planning, given the fact that it deprives him of all the richness contained in the variety of suggestions.

The strategic planning may be a good ally to achieve success, but it might also be the worst enemy.

The worst risk is to bureaucratize and transform the planning in a multiple conglomerate of deeds, information, memos, index cards, excessive meetings, etc.

Planning is a resource. It should never be a goal in itself. Planning teams are not justified just because they elaborate a plan. Their existence is useless if the plan does not bring real value to the organization.

If there is no answer to the question *"What value has the planning provided?"* or if the given answer is ambiguous, the best thing to do is to put the planning and the team that has elaborated it aside.

The best-known and most used method to elaborate an efficient strategic planning is the

SWOT method, named after, on the one hand, the analysis of the **S**trength and **W**eaknesses of the given organization and, on the other hand, the circumstances that the framework is offering us, materialized in **O**pportunities and **T**hreats derived from it.

The method begins with an evaluation of the Strong and Weak points of the organization, such as lack or availability of financial means, the type of existing management –creative or routine-like, enterprising or passive-, the human resources capacity, the human resources loyalty towards the company, the adequacy of the facilities and technology, etc.

Then, the next step is to make an evaluation of the present and predictable circumstances of the framework to see if there are Threats or Opportunities for the business in question.

For example:
- A larger market is an opportunity, but the possibility that it can attract new competitors is a threat
- A consolidated brand image is an opportunity for the production of a new line of products, taking advantage of that brand
- On the contrary, trying to create a new line of activity in a framework where there are already other efficient companies, represents a threat

- Having your own patent is an opportunity for creating a new line of activity
- The possibility that our main competitors create a consortium may be a threat
- Etc.

The SWOT method offers an excellent framework to think about the direction in which the organization must be led.

As examples of possible strategic decisions of a company for a certain period:
- Choosing the improvement of the annual profit level
- Choosing to increase the participation share in a certain market
- Choosing to reduce the products range and to focus on those in which the company is specialized or has a particular technological advantage
- Choosing to establish a partnership with one of the main competitors
- Etc.

After analyzing the Strong and Weak points and the Opportunities and Threats, the company may reach the point where it finds solid arguments from which to choose **the strategic lines** considered the most suitable ones.

For example, the SWOT analysis might lead us to the decision that our organization must focus now on obtaining a share of the market and leave the gain of economic profit for the coming years.

The SWOT method may be used in a similar way to adopt decisions in the public policies framework.

If the improvement of the passengers and freight exchange with a neighboring country were pursued, then carrying out a SWOT analysis would be advisable.

It should consider data such as geographic relief, the concentration or dissemination level of the population, the fleet of vehicles available in that country, the type of imported and exported products, etc in order to find out the advantages and disadvantages of the different possible strategies.

So, as an example of possible strategic decisions to improve the passengers and freight exchange with a neighboring country we have to mention:

- Choosing the development of the road net
- Choosing the development of the railway net
- Choosing the creation of an airport net
- Etc.

Thus, through SWOT we would have reflected about the things we wish to do considering both the features and capacities of the organization (or country) and the existing framework.

In addition to the strategic level, the planning must detail the objectives and formulate the action lines (programs) and actions (projects), which will allow the adopted strategic definition, to become a reality. Therefore, after defining the chosen strategy, the central goal or goals have to be determined. For example, to obtain a 10% market share in the first year, 20% in the second, and so on.

```
PLANNING ------------ PLANS

PROGRAMMING ------- PROGRAMS

DETAILING ---------- PROYECTS
```

Plans, programs and projects must be designed to allow the accomplishment of the chosen goals.

For example, an advertising campaign should be projected as a **plan**. Then, two **programs** could be included in the campaign, one on the radio and other in the written press. It should also give details about how to concrete the program through **projects**, such as an advertising space for three months in X channel or, alternatively various advertising spaces in channels X, Y and Z during one month.

Similarly, the Press program **may be** implemented by a **specialized** magazine, which could reach potential clients by the **general** information press or in any other way.

The necessary **means** for each project must be defined (budget, human resources, training, etc.) as well as the person or the unit in charge that will carry out or supervise the project.

Finally, it is necessary to establish some **indicators** that will allow the evaluation and establish the extent to which the project is accomplished (execution indicators) and has been effective (indicators of results).

This sequence of decisions will allow a complete Planning, which defines the results to be obtained, how to achieve them, the means assigned, and who the persons or units that should be responsible for each project and for the global overall goal expected are.

4.2 Management by Objectives

The Management by Objectives (MBO) is closely related to the Strategic Planning and it can even be said that the Strategic Planning is the brainchild of MBO.

The Strategic Planning is nothing more than an improved system for defining the objectives.

One of the main contributions of Peter Drucker[7] was to underline that one of the fundamental keys for any company's success is to know **what** the object of its business is, **what** its mission is, **what** its capacities are and **how** to keep its efforts focused on concrete objectives.

These statements, which today might seem obvious, were revolutionary in the 60's, when it was common for both public and private organizations to act based only on precedents, to react forced by the circumstances and to introduce innovations only by impulse.

At that time, not enough effort was made to plan the future and to define the concrete objectives that the company wished to accomplish.

Even today, the facts show that the management of many organizations devotes a bigger part of their thinking time to the question: *"**how** do we do this?"* and very little or no time at all to the question: *"**what** do we do?"*

---

[7] Peter Drucker (1990-2005) He is considered one of those who brought vision and suggestions regarding Organization Management Techniques

In 1954, Peter Drucker proposed MBO in his book *"The Practice of Management"* as a key for success in management. The essence of this technique, which he took up again and developed later in other publications, consisted of underlining that the manager must:
- Set the objectives clearly
- Structure the organization in units, which will be able to accomplish objectives
- Set objectives for each unit
- Control the accomplished results and compare them with those that had been foreseen.

The new Management by Objectives (MBO) proposes **a change in the old management style**, which mainly consists of giving orders and instructions to the employees to carry out certain tasks.

Instead, MBO considers that the managing team has to:
- **Define** what must be done
- **Point out** which units or, work teams, are responsible for each program or project
- **Give** them autonomy to organize themselves with the assigned means
- **Supervise** to what extent the results foreseen in the definition of objectives are being achieved by the Unts in charge of them.

The planning technique SWOT and the Management By Objectives (MBO) should:
- **Generate** a product consisting of a Strategy, Plans, Programs and Projects
- **Follow** the execution of the Plan and MBO
- **Evaluate** the results

We could assume that two organizations applying these techniques would carry out a similar management style.

However, the reality of the organizations shows that there are **very substantial differences** in the management styles, mainly derived from **the way** each organization implements the SWOT, **how** it elaborates the MBO and **how** it puts it into practice.

The main differences reside in **who is invited** to define the objectives and make the planning and to what extent these people **are, or are not, empowered** to make decisions. That gives way to different management styles, and involves managers and employees in a very different way.

The management style exercises a large influence on managers and employees when it comes to the acceptance and commitment to achieve the established Objectives.

4.3 Risks of the strategic planning and MBO

One of the major risks of the Planning processes is to intend an exaggerated perfectionism and, especially, to **transform the Planning,** which is a mean, **in a goal in itself.**

Sometimes, the complexity of the procedure, its insistence regarding insignificant details and, especially, its bureaucratization, transforms the planning in an obstacle for the organization dynamism.

Sometimes the process kills the management efficiency. That happens when we give more importance to the process than to the product itself.

Mintzberg[8] launched some of the hardest criticisms against Jelinek, who was fascinated by the *"goals, tactics and strategies"* system of Texas Instruments, a new planning method at that time.

Nevertheless, one of the Texas Instruments managers later described that method using terms which were not praiseworthy: *"paper factory that makes absolutely impossible to react to any object that is moving quickly"*.

---

[8] Henry Mintzberg (born in 1939), professor of the McGill University from Montreal (Canada) His most well-known works are the Nature of the Management Work and the Organizations' Structure

Years later, Texas Instruments modified radically its planning style. It was transformed into a more flexible tool focused on stimulating the organization and not on controlling it.

In the same direction, the words of the famous expert in political sciences, Aaron **Wildawsky,** must be quoted. He exclaimed in 1973 *"the more, the worst",* regarding the elaborated and complex planning processes[9] introduced in the public sector by Robert McNamara, when he was USA's Defense State Secretary.

Ricardo **Semler**[10], in his excellent book entitled *"Radical",* writes about his experience as a manager and explains the evolution that his own management conception went through. He says that he passed from a management conception focused on a very detailed and centralized planning to a great autonomy and decentralization, both of the planning and of the management itself.

---

[9] From his PPBS (Planning Programing Budgeting System) derived the generalization of Budget by Programs

[10] In the 80ies, Ricardo Semler, young and dynamic Brazilian businessman, introduced in his company revolutionary changes in management, based on units not bigger than 100 workers, endowed with autonomy and responsibility, both in production decisions and remuneration ones

Mintzberg made the following observation: *"It's not that the planning simply does not work; it could be even very dangerous".* **This statement is as drastic as it is true.** In many cases, the planning becomes a goal in itself, which justifies the creation of planning teams (and the subsequent payment of their wages), that generate multiple ideas formulated rigidly, almost as immutable truths.

This rigid approach reduces the power of the management, preventing it from flexibly adapting itself to the environment changes and limits excessively the autonomy that the managers need in order to run the units of the organization.

Planning **must be a flexible** framework that makes it possible for the management to adequate its decisions to a changing reality. That does not mean that the manager can act letting aside the Plan, but that the Plan should present certain flexibility and be reviewed in an agile way.

Planning is a suitable and **adequate tool to create a reflection and forecast processes,** which undoubtedly is part of the management tasks. Nevertheless, there are **four important mistakes,** which must be avoided:

- Create **big teams** exclusively dedicated to planning
- Devote **excessive time** to planning

- Use **too sophisticated and complex** processes, which means using multiple files, memoranda, etc
- Consider the Plan as a **compulsory rigid guideline,** that must be accomplished to its smallest details, or that requires procedures so complicated to modify that, in the end, are unmodifiable.

As an **efficient** planning method, the manager of a large company or organization should:

- Include in the planning activity both the **executing and the think-tank staff**. Ask the persons, who will participate in the planning, to prepare their ideas previously and succinctly.
- Have small groups (two or three people each) interact and perform an initial **brainstorming session** and draw conclusions (it isn't necessary to reach a consensus)
- Organize a general meeting of the core-planning group (with no more than 10 people) that should last no longer than two days, to analyze the aforementioned conclusions and write **a simple and clear document** containing the plan draft with its foreseen objectives and actions.

- Ask anyone in the organization that could contribute with valuable suggestions for their opinions regarding the plan draft document. Ask anyone else who has shown real interest in expressing ideas and opinions.
- Elaborate the final detailed plan, considering, in this case, those new contributions.

Obviously, a small company or organization should reduce radically both the number of people and the time dedicated to planning.

Anyway, all the planning process, regardless of the size of the organization, should apply the following **guidelines**:

- Consider the employees as a great source of suggestions.
- Offer them the possibility to make proposals, explaining them.
- Assume their proposals, or exclude them explaining why.
- Have clear, right from the beginning, that the plan should be elaborated within a reasonable time.

Any excellent planning effort must implicate and motivate the employees. The planning is only an instrument to achieve three main aims: **foreseeing** the future, **adapting** to changes and **adjusting** the means to the expected objectives.

Excellence Management does not oppose the Strategic Planning, or the Management by Objectives. It considers these as very profitable techniques or tools, but under **two absolute necessary conditions**:

1. Planning and defining projects and actions have to be **dynamic, flexible and revisable at any moment**. They should never be a rigid tool that prevents the introduction of improvements.

2. **The employees should be invited to participate**, to a reasonable extent, in the planning process and in the definition of the responsibilities of the employees and Units. The door should be always clearly open to the employee's suggestions. **The employee's talents are not to be despised**.

5 ORGANIZATIONAL STRUCTURE

It is necessary to establish a process for reaching a goal. If this process needs the collaboration of several individuals, an organization will have to be created. That requires defining the competences and tasks that each one will have to carry out so as to generate the final products and services.

Any organization aims to produce services or goods. They can be very different as far as material products are concerned, such as food, chairs, etc or as far as intangible products are concerned, like entertainment activities or human relations training, etc.

Every product or service, be it a vehicle or an opera concert, is always generated through more or less standardized processes, consisting of different phases that aim at obtaining that product or service.

In many cases, the large conceptual scope of the objective that must be achieved requires the itemization of the concept (for example, the improvement of the road and railway transport infrastructure) into more concrete programs (railway and road programs). In addition, these programs will be broken down into further concrete projects, which will define what we really want to produce (for example, to improve the road between town A and town B or the train connection between town M and town N).

Then, those products and services that appear in the plan must be materialized.
At that moment, it is necessary to go from the idea to the action, from the plan to its execution, from the project to its implementation.

That is why **an organizational framework has to be established**: who does what, what ability everyone performs, who is in charge of coordination and control, how the different parts of the organization communicate, etc.
Any organization dedicated to business, or other activities, is made up of units formed by individuals. In fact, hardly ever is an organization created to perform a plan. Normally the plan is made under the consideration that there is already a certain organizational structure.
However, no organizational structure or organizational chart can be an obstacle to the achievement of the goals.
No organizational structure or organizational chart **may be sacred *per se*.** If the organizational structure blocks the efficient functioning of the organization, the mission accomplishment, **the leader should feel entitled to modify it**.

```
┌─────────────────────────────────────────┐
│                              Organizational │
│   Mission ──▶ Activities ──▶   Structure    │
└─────────────────────────────────────────┘
```

We may go even further: It is an excellent challenge for any organization **to rethink** its own organizational structure **periodically**.

Bill Gates, founder of Microsoft, stressed that he turns the company upside down once every two or three years, as a way of keeping it dynamic and creative. In the same way that elections are organized at a fixed date every few years, it wouldn't be a bad idea for the organizations, public or private, to undertake the commitment of rethinking themselves periodically, for example once every three years.

There are two main traditional organizational structures: **functional** (or process structure) or structure **by products**.

In the **functional** structure, each body carries out a certain phase, or process, and the combination of all of them generates the final products.

In the structure **by products,** each body or section produces a range of final products.

Around these directly productive Units there are other supporting Units that are in charge of accountability, human resources, maintenance, etc.

Nowadays, the trend of structuring by products predominates, which allows for more autonomy and, subsequently, greater responsibility for each Unit.

There is **not any type** of organizational design (by phases, processes or products) that could be considered the **ideal for all** organizations and companies. It depends on the circumstances of each case.

The **organizational structure depends mostly on the activity** that it must carry out.
It is not the same to manufacture cars as to make tailored suits. In the first case, a more complex process is needed, in which different specialist workers participate in an assembling line; while, in the second case, only one person may make the suits.
In the same way, it is obvious that the work organization in a lawyer's office is very different from the one we can find in an ironworks plant.

The **technological progress** (the introduction of robots and new machines that replace and facilitate man's work) leads to the redistribution of tasks and processes that are carried out by each worker in the organization.

Besides, nowadays, it is possible to notice an upward trend in terms of connecting the worker to the final product (the product he helps to produce) to make him feel more connected to the achieved results and -to a greater degree- more responsible.

There is a basic organizational principle: any organization that aims at being successful must be focused on its main mission. The **central core** of its organizational structure must be **dedicated to produce** its main products or services.

Although this may seem obvious**, it does not always happen in real life**. On the contrary, you may easily notice, especially in the large organizations, that those bodies that carry out the supporting tasks (administrative, accountability, advising, planning, etc.) have a dangerous trend of growing disproportionately, when compared to the rest of the organization.

All this generates excessive, unproductive, and bureaucratic unestimulating indirect costs, which influence the final costs of the goods and services and thus harm the results account.

That is why the existence of each body, unit or task in the organization must always be rationally justified.

From the organization's point of view, the manager must constantly ask himself to what extent each body, unit or task adds value to the final production of the organization.

In other words, to what degree the organization's final production would be affected if the dimensions of a body, unit or task were reduced. **Each body, unit or task should be really productive**.

Total Quality Management or Excellence Philosophy encourages all the employees and units to generate value and to evolve in this direction. Consequently, it considers that the units and the employees themselves must be a natural source of suggestions.

Those suggestions must provide adaptations and changes in the organizational structure oriented to eliminate unproductive costs and to guarantee that all the resources generate value.

Employment stability stimulates the employee's collaboration in the reorganization process. If they are worried about the risk of being fired, they probably will not cooperate.

There is not a simple type of organizational structure that may be considered, in a general sense, more efficient than others. Neither the functional structure, nor the processes structure; neither the structure by products, nor the holding structure are the most adequate structure for all cases.

The truly 'avant-garde' or revolutionary structure is the one that considers itself provisional and is open not only to be revised from the outside but is also **ready to "rethink itself" periodically from within.**

6 THE DIRECTOR AS STAFF MANAGER

One of the traditional definitions of leadership is *"the condition that a person has that enables him **to obtain results through other people"***. This definition emphasizes the leader[11], the director, the manager's nature as a mobilizer (someone who promotes an action) of the human resources more than his abilities to exercise the functions of planning or defining the organization's mission.

It is good to remember that it is essential to achieve the staff's involvement in the planning and in the formulation of suggestions, if we expect the employees to mobilize and commit themselves.

The director's function, as staff manager, is essential and its efficient realization requires taking into consideration four basic aspects:

1. The director's natural qualities
2. The director's acquired qualities
3. The characteristics of the organization
4. The staff's interests and motivations

---

[11] In this book, "Excellence in Management" the terms leader, director, managers are used in general as synonyms

6.1 The manager's natural qualities

By the manager's **natural qualities,** we understand his character and personality features:
- Physical features, such as energy, height, appearance.
- Intelligence
- Personality features, such as adaptability, aggressiveness, enthusiasm and self-esteem.
- Features related to the task to be carried out, such as the desire for success, perseverance and initiative.
- Social features like cooperation, interpersonal relations and management skills.

It is convenient to clarify that from the point of view of natural qualities, there is not only one model of leadership. Certain leaders have natural qualities while others have other types of qualities. It should be underlined that even the possession of several natural qualities does not guarantee a good leadership.

All **natural** features and those that are acquired during a person's lifetime, are **deeply rooted** in the person and will naturally appear in the way the leader manages their staff. The natural qualities are a profound and well-consolidated substratum of a person. It is impossible, or very difficult, to change them in a medium-term period.

Every manager must be **aware** of what we could call their *"way of **being**"* and must avoid pretending to be *"**someone else**"* all of a sudden. This does not mean that he must accept that to change some facets of his personality is an impossible task. However, he must be aware of the fact that many of them can be modified only with a lot of effort, and just in a medium or long term.

The manager must emphasize his strong natural points and look for collaborators who could improve his weak points. He must reflect about what activities are more adequate to his natural qualities. He must keep in mind that for these activities he has a natural advantage regarding other leaders.

A good manager should accept life as a constant evolution and learning process. He must be aware that some of his qualities will be important at a certain moment and others at a different moment or circumstance.

6.2 Manager's acquired abilities

Even more important than the manager's character and personality are the **management abilities acquired** through training and experience.

Among those abilities, we should first mention one's own **capacity to understand what leadership means**. In this sense, it is worthwhile reading the conclusions drawn by various authors, such as Robert Blake, Jane Mouton, Likert, Tannenbaum, Hersey-Blanchard, Fiedler, etc. in their studies on the leadership concept.

These authors' ideas, conclusions and differences in their approach to the concept of leadership can help the manager to better understand which type of leadership is more appropriate for his organization.

The concrete abilities for the **labor organization,** like the ones offered by the new technologies (electronic agenda, e-mail, videoconference, etc) open new horizons for the manager. Knowing the potential of these new tools, the manager can orient and guide his staff to use them in order to do a more **efficient** work.

The knowledge of **idea-generating and decision-making techniques**, such as *brainstorming*, the nominal group technique, the hat system, etc. allow the manager to use them during staff meetings, introducing in this way innovative abilities in the organization management **culture**.

Of course, **training is not enough** to develop leadership abilities. We must recall here the saying *"human beings explain what they know and teach others what they are"'*. We are the fruit of what we learn, internalize and put into practice.

Leadership abilities are acquired through experience. **Only the experience** of leadership abilities allows the leader to understand both his potential and limitations, and the difficulties and the advantages that may arise from the use of those abilities.

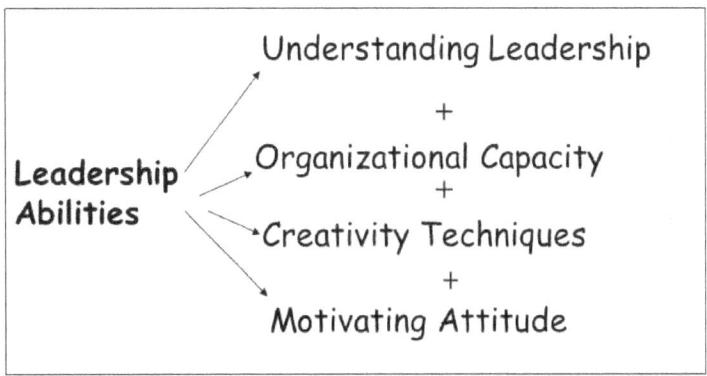

One of the main characteristics of a leader is his **innovative capacity**. The main difference between the concept of a leader and a manager is similar to the difference between Christopher Columbus and the commander of a ship that is frequently sailing a regular line. Both of them, run a ship, but Columbus was in charge of taking a lot more diverse and innovative decisions than the captain of a regular line ship, whose decisions are taken right from the start of the voyage.

This does not mean that the captain of a ship does not have room to be a leader, and that he will only see himself as a mere manager. The ship commander can as well manage the staff in a creative way. He can make innovations in the processes and the way of managing life on board (passengers and crew); he can also create and apply new methods with respect to other procedures, such as embarking and disembarking, etc.

Only **if he tries to innovate, will he be acting as a leader.** If he does not do it that way, he will act like the manager of a complex organization, like the manager of complex and independent processes, but not as a real leader.

The term leader is similar to that of driver. The leader uses new ways, leads towards new objectives. Any professional that wishes to be not just a manager but also a leader must take into consideration the fact that the leader plays the role of **a profound transformer of the organization**, in all its facets: employees, processes, products; and he can even change or redesign the organization's mission.

One of the leader's most difficult challenges is his **role as a transformer of his own employees**. A real leader encourages his employees to become new leaders. He is aware of the risk of losing his employees due to the training they have received, as they may leave the organization or may even take over the leader's job position. This risk can become a matter of concern for the leader. Nevertheless, a real leader should get over those worries, as he is also aware of his own knowledge, experience, capacities and value.

On the other hand, the leader **must conceive the world as a relational world** in which, the fact that people, who worked and were trained under his guidance, come to assume leadership positions in his organization or elsewhere, can be profitable, both for him and his leadership recognition. Indeed, they will be **witnesses of his leadership capacities**.

Certainly, the employees might be aware of the leader's weaknesses and limitations as well, and they could use them against him, from inside or outside the company.

However, in the end, what is most important is the leader's **personal balance**.

Every manager should ask himself: *"In my style of leadership, what is more important: My strong or my weak points? Do I really agree with my own way of leading the organization?"*

The leader's **self-confidence**, based on his **accomplishments**, (*"by their fruits you will acknowledge them"*) and assessed as objectively as possible, is definitely his main foundation to move on.

6.3 The organization characteristics

The manager's possibilities of action are more or less limited by the nature of the organization, namely by the type of products or services it generates.

Tom Burns and G.M. Stalker have studied 20 English enterprises and have discovered a very clear concordance between the organizational style and the context in which the company operates. They noticed the existence of two basic organizational models that were applied regularly in various organizations.

One of these models was called **MECHANISTIC**. It seemed the most adequate and frequent in relatively stable and defined contexts.

The MECHANISTIC style is characterized by:
- differentiation of specialized tasks between individuals and units

- individuals that believed that their tasks are different from those of the rest of the members in the organization
- well-defined rights and obligations
- well-defined hierarchical structure
- vertical interaction between the superior and the subordinates
- functioning based on instructions and decisions that come from the superior

The other model that they studied, called **ORGANIC**, was usually found in organizations that confronted unstable and changing situations, or problems whose solution could not be forecast or standardized, and had to be adapted to the circumstances specific to each case.

The organizational ORGANIC style was characterized by:
- Individual development based on the knowledge of the different types of tasks of all the other members in the organization
- Continuous redefinition of the tasks through the interaction with the others
- Intense interaction and coordination to adopt decisions and to attain objectives.

Briefly, the ORGANIC style is characterized by a greater polyvalence, staff rotation and an important horizontal communication, whereas the MECHANISTIC style is characterized by a special focus on the specialization in a certain job and the observance of the very precise instructions that normally come from a superior or are established by him at the beginning.

Continuing with this type of studies, **Joan Woodward** found out a relation between the technological complexity of the enterprises and the organizational model they usually adopt. His studies, carried out in 100 English enterprises, produced a **classification of three groups**, according to their production type:
  a) Production by request, in small quantities
  b) Mass and large quantity production
  c) Production at a continuous process or flow, as the one used in chemical enterprises or oil refineries

Classified this way, she noticed that the most efficient and prosperous enterprises of the **groups a) and c)** had the tendency to have an **ORGANIC** organizational style whereas the most efficient and prosperous enterprises of **group b)** were inclined to adopt the **MECHANISTIC** organizational style.

When the structure of the organization is MECHANISTIC, as is the case of an enterprise whose productive process operates through assembly chains, **the leader's possibilities to** transform processes, redistribute functions among the staff members and facilitate the reception of the suggestions are much more reduced as the production process cannot be interrupted.

In such cases, experimental innovations cannot be introduced very easily. In the cases in which they are introduced, this will happen only after a careful process of reflection and trying not to affect the production line too much.

On the contrary, if the enterprise focuses on fulfilling orders by request, designing new products and seeking solutions for new situations, the manager's role as a transformer meets a more adequate environment to apply his creativity.

In this context, any new project, any new task represents a new occasion for the reorganization of the organizational chart and for the outlining of new objectives for the staff working in that organization.

In the Public Administration, **the services delivery bodies**, (such as the case of a Provincial Traffic Bureau[12]) normally have a well-regulated structure, in which each unit is attributed the

---

[12] Authority responsible for monitoring traffic, the issuance of driver's licenses and the registration of vehicles ownership. One of its functions is the allocation and the registration of the car plates after the reception and verification of the necessary documentation

execution of **concrete processes**, phases or services.

This reality limits, to a certain extent, the leader's possibilities to introduce profound and frequent changes within the organization, as the existing processes define the natural organization structure.

On the contrary, the **design or study bodies** have a more flexible structure in which the employees of the technical department distribute among themselves the tasks depending on the priorities.

In this case, the activities are carried out most of the time **by a team** and a natural recycling of the staff is done depending on the type of studies or work tasks they have been entrusted with.

Anyway, **all organizations can evolve and innovate**, all processes can be modified and the rigidity of a certain type of organization, such as the MECHANISTIC, does not prevent the leader from fulfilling his obligations regarding the evolution (improvement and innovation) of the organization and processes in order to obtain high efficiency, efficacy and quality quotas.

There are always possibilities to apply one's creativity, to realize processes of functional studies and to introduce improvements. In order to do that it is very helpful to bring out the natural talent of the staff who is placed in different jobs. These talents are a great source of creativity for the organizational development.

The leader must be aware that the nature of the activity within the organization, be it in a *'mechanical' or 'organic'* context, limits his possible leadership style to a certain extent. As far as we can see, it is not the same to lead an army during a war than to run a group of teachers in a university in times of peace.

Excellence in Management will not imply the same management style in a mass production enterprise as in another that generates services by request, **but its main management principles and techniques will remain the same.**

Introducing Excellent Management **implies choosing a revolutionary, innovative and permanent management**, as we shall explain later.

The director or manager will always have the possibility to implement Excellent Management, although **its functioning in its external manifestations will be different** from one case to another, from an Organic company to a Mechanistic one.

6.4 Staff's interests and motivation

The staff's interests and motivations condition the type of leadership that the manager can adopt. It is obviously not the same to run a monastery, an assembly section of an industrial company or a university. The personnel in each of these cases will surely have different motivations.

Motivation is a general term applied to any type of impulses, desires, needs and aspirations. **Motivation makes one act** with the hope of achieving a result, and from the result satisfaction will derive.

In an enterprise, a person may feel very motivated **to act. However,** that does not guarantee that he gets enough satisfaction from his work. This could be either because of lack of self-realization or because of economic interests that are not satisfied. In such a case, this person **may try to leave** the organization.

Just the opposite can happen when a person feels, on one hand, satisfied with the recognition, prestige and salary he gets from the organization, **but,** on the other hand, **has a weak motivation to act.** Consequently, he will not be a productive factor for the organization. In this case, the organization **will try to get rid of this person.**

Motivations are subjective and circumstantial and may come **from our internal** self (aspirations, personal desires, etc) and **from external** influences, such as the type of management or other circumstances.

The motivational equilibrium is reached when the internal and external impulses are kept at a reasonable proportion. In other words, what the individual gets from the organization (payment, professional satisfaction, human relations) will turn into motivation **if his internal value system is satisfied.**

Besides, the activity of the manager has great importance for both the **creation** of new motivations among the staff (for example, the desire of professional success) and for their **satisfaction**.

Sometimes the facet of the manager as a **creator of motivations** is forgotten. It is usually considered that the staff should already know what their motivations are and that the role of the leader is just to respond to them at a greater or smaller extent. This interpretation is completely wrong.

In many cases, the staff *"believes"* that the only motivational factor is a **salary** raise when, in reality, what probably satisfies them most is the **recognition** they get from the management and their colleagues.

Many times the staff is not aware of the existence of other motivations different from the ones that had been obvious so far. Thus, there are cases in which the sole economic motivation (in the sales domain, for example) can be replaced, at least partially, by guarantees related to a career (for example, the fact that the person turns into a local manager or regional sales manager).

In other cases, the commitment of the staff towards the organization can be consolidated when the staff is treated with more consideration, when their suggestions and opinions are heard, etc.
Motivation does not always come from additional money bonuses.

Anyway, it is also true that the leader can create new motivational lines, **but they cannot substitute the elementary aspirations** that the staff already has.

If the staff has certain relevant economic needs, due to personal or family reasons, it will be useless for the leader to request more collaboration from them —only appealing to their love for the country. This type of exceptional motivational line (love for the country) can function but just for short periods of time.

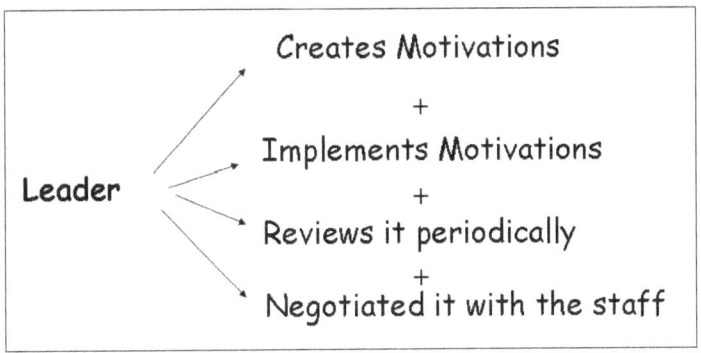

A leader **should not expect to create a motivational scale accepted unanimously** by all the staff, as every person has their own circumstances and particular motivational scale.

Nevertheless, the leader's ideas regarding the motivational elements of the staff can penetrate, **if well communicated**, and, as time passes by, **become a cultural characteristic** of that organization. Of course, the staff that does not agree with the new motivational culture will leave the organization step by step.

Obviously, **the consequences of a new motivational scale**, such as
- weaker or more intense collaboration of the staff
- lower or higher productivity
- employees drain towards other organizations
- requests for engagement at our organization
- etc,

will show the leader **whether the scale** of the motivations he has created **is beneficial or not** for the organization.

In addition, the leader must take into consideration the fact that there is not a unique scale of motivations, which is the most adequate in every case and circumstance.

He must be aware that the **revision and modification of the motivational elements** from time to time can represent a revolutionary factor within the organization, contributing to avoid monotony and stagnation.

Due to this reason, the leader must not be afraid to introduce, at a certain moment, a bonus for performance and cancel it a few years later.

However, these decisions **must be well grounded** so that the staff understands why they are introduced.

It is necessary **to avoid arbitrary decisions** taken just to keep with the trend of the moment or because of a hidden agenda.

An essential characteristic of any motivational system to be motivating **is its acceptance** by all the staff, or at least by most of the employees.

Negotiating and reaching consensus on the motivational scale is a good way to move forward but, **in any case, the final and global**

responsibility of leading an organization **is in the manager's hands**.

6.5 Main staff motivation theories

The scholars have pointed out the existence of different motivation scales.

One of the most well-known is the one proposed by **Abraham Maslow**[13] who signalized the existence of an individual motivation scale that he named the *"Hierarchy of Needs"*. It is the following, in an ascending order:

1. **Physiological** needs. These needs are the ones that correspond to the satisfaction of the basic needs of human life, such as food, water, heat, clothing and sleep. Maslow pointed out that while these needs are not satisfied there will be no other superior needs that can motivate people.
2. **Safety** needs. They refer to not having the fear of losing one's job, property, food, protection, etc...
3. **Affiliation or acceptance** needs. People, as social beings, feel the need for belonging and being accepted by others.

---

[13] Abraham Maslow (1908-1970) Human behavior psychologist. Teacher at the University of Massachusetts (USA)

4. **Esteem** needs. The feeling of belonging is not enough. It is necessary to feel self-respect and respected by others. People want to obtain satisfactions such as power, status, prestige, affection and self-confidence.
5. **Self-realization** needs. They correspond to the desire of "*being*", in its philosophical sense. That is, expressing our potential in its totality.

Maslow's theories were questioned by other researchers who stated that we cannot talk about the existence of a hierarchy or order of necessities.

They pointed out that individuals, who do not fulfill their first and second level needs explained by Maslow, can be motivated by other needs of another scale. It means that there is no absolute hierarchy of needs. The fact that the needs vary in intensity from one individual to another was also noted.

Peter Drucker, in his book *"Administration: Tasks, Responsibilities and Practices"* wrote that Maslow has not taken into account that *"every need changes in the very moment it has been satisfied"*

Another prestigious author regarding the motivational elements was **Friedrich Herzberg**.

He stated that in the context of a labor organization, there are **two main motivational factors**:

1. **Hygiene** factors
2. Strictly **motivational** factors

As **hygiene** factors, Herzberg mentioned:
- Work conditions
- Interpersonal relations
- Salary, status
- Safety at the working place
- Safety for personal life

Herzberg claims that if these factors are not available, or do not exist, people will not be satisfied. Nevertheless, **their existence does not guarantee satisfaction as well**.

As strictly **motivational** factors, Herzberg mentioned the following:
- Working with challenges
- Success
- Professional and personal development
- Responsibility
- Professional career
- Recognition for the good work done

According to him, these factors create the employee's motivation. He proposed a fundamental line of motivation called "**job enrichment**", which means to expand the contents of a job position, to attribute more responsibility to a job position -both in managing and in creativity- and the existence of a professional career.

The way to obtain the *"job enrichment"* consists of:

- guaranteeing the employee a higher degree of **freedom** in decision-making regarding aspects such as the methods, the procedures and the pace of work
- increasing the degree of **participation** and interaction between the employees
- maintaining an agile **exchange** of suggestions, opinions and answers between the manager and the employees

In the "job enrichment" process, the differences between the individuals must be taken into account.

We must **avoid falling into the trap** of believing that *"what I like he will like"* as not all individuals want the same quota of participation and responsibility. For example, for an extrovert employee the enhancement of the public relation degree of his job can be extremely motivating, whereas for an introvert employee this could be a real sacrifice.

Consequently, the enrichment of a job must be done in different ways depending on who occupies the job position.

Other authors proposed other points of view with respect to motivation.

Victor Vroom proposed the **expectancy theory**. He pointed out that people will be motivated to do certain things and achieve certain objectives if they are convinced of the value of those objectives and if they believe that all they do will contribute to the achievement of them.

Vroom believes that the individual motivation is the result of the value that he assigns to the expected result, multiplied by the confidence (expectancy) in that his efforts will contribute to the achievement of the result:

Motivation = value x expectancy

The higher the value an individual gives to a type of reward and the greater expectations he has that his actions will contribute to reaching that reward, the more he is motivated.

Thus, a certain economic reward for sales is even more motivating the higher the employee's expectancies in reaching that level of sales are. If he believes that it is almost impossible to reach that level, his motivation in reaching it will be almost null.

The same thing will happen if his expectancies of reaching the expected level of sales are high but the value of the economic reward (due to its low quantity or other circumstances) is low.

Obviously, the same result (Ex. a concrete reward) has different value to different individuals because it depends on each individual's scale of values. For some, a determined type of reward may have a lesser value than for others.

In practice, in organizations **that claim to be long lasting**, such as big companies and public organizations, Herzberg's proposal[14] seems to be adequate. Money is not everything. The possibilities for a career, being listened to, participating, achieving self-realization, etc. have also a great and important role in staff motivation.

On the contrary, actions in which the individual takes part only **sporadically**, when there is no career future or where the result depends mainly on individual effort (sales, consultancy, etc.) the motivational element normally is an **immediate economic reward**, for we never know what can happen tomorrow.

This is also the case of organizations, or units, created to develop a concrete project or work, that will close down once their objectives

---

[14] As we shall see, Total Quality opts for this type of motivation

have been achieved. In these cases, the economic factor frequently represents the main motivational factor.

Every manager wants his **organization to be enduring**, even if he admits that profound changes could happen in the future. A leader should not omit the fact that his organization might change its profile later on, in which case he may need to re-orient it towards other productive activities, and may be forced to shut down some specialized units.

However, he always **hopes that a relatively stable nucleus** within the organization **will still exist** in the future. In this stable nucleus, that can include an important part of the organization's Units, the motivation approach proposed by Herzberg seems to be very adequate.

Loyalty based on mere economic motivation is very unstable and does not facilitate transparency and cooperation. On the contrary, it invites the members of the organization to hide information, referring both to data and to technologies, so that they keep a greater number of aces in their hands to be indispensable to the organization, minimizing the risk of being dismissed.

In case of self-employment, the economic factor is an important motivation but the same goes for personal satisfaction and especially for the achievement of a respected *"brand image"*.

This brand is a guarantee that, in the future, the regular and the new clients will be attracted by the good name of the self-employee, and will request their professional services.

7 AFTER THEORY COMES PRACTICE

Following the considerations exposed in the previous pages, the manager can ask himself:

- To plan: how and to what extent?
- To set objectives: how?
- To establish, revise and modify the organizational structure: how?
- To design and improve production processes: how?
- To design new products: how?
- To evaluate the production levels reached: how?
- The staff motivation: with what means?
- Etc.

Reality proves that although these issues are fundamental to turn a normal enterprise into a successful one, quite often the manager, overwhelmed by everyday work, does not give a systematic and structured answer to them.

Only when the emergency of a situation imposes it, or in face of a crisis, does the manager **give answers** to those previous questions, **often improvising,** depending on his character and professional knowledge and experiences.

In other cases, he might choose **to meet his closest collaborators** and together try to find answers that should then be implemented.

He can also use the help of the **external consultants** who will offer him ideas and suggestions, which can represent a valuable contribution. But he may still wonder: **How do I apply** them?

These are **the three** ways which a manager usually adopts when implementing new management formulas, in order to renew his organization.

Indeed the manager chooses, consciously or not, among various leadership philosophies or attitudes, more or less personal, more or less based on a hierarchic structure, more or less bureaucratic, more or less open to participation and consultation.

In this book we want to present, as clearly as possible, a **leadership philosophy named** Total Quality Management (TQM), **nowadays EXCELLENCE to the reader.** It offers concrete and deep reflections and answers to the most important questions related to the organization or leadership techniques that a manager may formulate.

It also includes the pillars of Excellence in Management, an integral and harmonized **pack of action lines and controls** that facilitates the implementation of this philosophy. They also serve to check whether the implementation has been done correctly and, if not, how to reorient it.

Excellence or TQM represents a management approach that we consider not only more complete but also more solid than other approaches, such as *reengineering*, *the leadership centered on the boss*, *the top-down creative impulse*, etc. The aforementioned approaches can create positive results in a short term but in general tend to be unstable and dangerous in a medium and long term.

Excellence or TQM is superior to this wide range of recipes that both Tom Peters in *Reinventing Excellence* and other authors proposed and that usually consists of an enumeration of varied and volatile cases from which it is difficult to draw a general conclusion. These recipes are very different from the Excellence.

It is frequent that, after reading some best-sellers in management issues, managers find it difficult to prioritize between a vast and varied panorama of suggestions. These are often quite unstable and fade away very quickly. Two thirds of the enterprises qualified in 1982 by Tom Peters as excellent became at a medium term ruined, according to Woolridge in *Mentors' Hour*. And this keeps happening in the XXI century.

Excellence in Management does not remain at the philosophical level or on that of great principles, but it explains the way in which these principles must be applied.

Moreover, it promotes the development of methodologies that allow the evaluation of the functioning of the various aspects of the organization (management, staff, results, etc.) and the evaluation of the extent at which the organization's management is coherent with the Excellence in Management proposal.

Excellence in Management implies taking into consideration not only the **WHAT** (the mission) but also the **HOW** (the processes) and the **WITH** (the resources).

It also focuses on getting **RESULTS** through the interaction and harmonization of the three types of fundamental agents existing in any organization: the **manager**, the **employees**, including the suppliers as indirect employees, and the **consumers** or end-users of the products and services.

SECTION II

EXCELLENCE OR TOTAL QUALITY

8 THE QUALITY CONCEPT

8.1 A concept often misunderstood

Human beings frequently expect, or so it seems, to find the Elixir Prodigy, the Magic Word whose mere utterance will transform reality in a wonderful and perfect scenario.

There is nothing wrong with wishing to achieve perfection. The wrong thing is to believe that it is possible to find a methodology, a tool, an automatic process that can make the organization function like a clock or to transform it, now and forever, in a perfect and unchanging Paradise.

This aspiration of finding the instrument, or the perfect system, forgets, on the one hand, the incidence of the different personalities of the organization's members and their hierarchical positions. On the other hand, it ignores that interactions with the environment (physical, social and economic) cause **constant change** in the activity, structure and functioning of organizations.

However, to say that there is not one single, perfect and immutable system to lead the organizations **should not be interpreted as saying** that it is not possible to find the basic principles for an efficient and modern leadership, able to lead the organization to success. It is possible. Then, here is where the different opinions and theories on organization and management find their value and reason for existence.

When searching for principles, analyzing them and offering solutions, it is very frequent to come across many new terminologies. This generates confusion and confirms the statement that sometimes *"cannot see the forest for the trees".*

New terms such as excellence, total quality management, strategic planning, reengineering, program budget, zero-based budgeting, change management, knowledge management, emotional intelligence, scorecard, etc. arise continually.

All these proposals or tools are not bad per se and can even be inspiring. Unfortunately, when formulated in an ambiguous, unclear or incomplete way it becomes difficult to grasp their essence, understand their specific contents and, in particular, how different they are from previous approaches in use.

The coincidence, in time and space, of **various proposals** of management styles, creates an excellent breeding ground where **confusion can take root** and proliferate. The feeling that "*no sooner the first message has been received and understood than the second one is already* *approaching"* can be **good for academics but maddening for managers**.

Terry Neil[15], director of the Change Management section in Andersen Consulting, summarizing an internal study of his own organization, noted that one of the main reasons for the failure in the efforts to renew the company was "***death by a thousand initiatives***".

Literally, he says that in business, it **often happens** that *"the training program on Tuesday, the total quality management on Wednesday, reengineering on Thursday and the concept of "apprentice company on Friday"* are implanted.

Then, he affirms: *"all these ideas are very important, but when they are thrown at the employees as tennis aces, they become overwhelmed and confused, and the focus of the company becomes blurred."*

Does this mean that Terry Neil is against the study and learning of new methodologies and tools? No, it does not.

He means that the fundamental attitude is not to search for recipes or methods but primarily **to capture the spirit** and the principles that inspire those suggestions for improvements. **It is necessary to become the owners of the tools, not just their servants**.

---

[15] See "The Pursuit of Wow" Tom Peters. 1994

We cannot innovate one day with a tool and then the next day with another, because we would be contributing to create confusion among the employees in regards to where we want to go and **how we can get there.**

Therefore the manager must choose and adopt a management philosophy and a methodology that allows him to assess if the goals and the means are coordinated and working properly. Of course, he should be open to modify or even replace his management philosophy and methodology, but until he does so, he must be clear about what management technique he is using and why.

Excellence or Total Quality Management is the specific management style we stand for. We must emphasize that very often the real meaning of TQM is not always perceived in the same way. What are we for: Quality of Management or Management of Quality?

This gives room to various interpretations, which in some cases are far from the original purpose and spirit of Total Quality Management. The **first challenge** that arises is, therefore, **to clarify** what Total Quality or Excellence in Management means.

Unfortunately, reality shows that many people who attend courses in Total Quality do not understand its essence and often only retain its title and some of the side stories or techniques that were presented.

Moreover, they often allude to Deming as a promoter of the statistical process control.

That is correct but it blurs the essence of his message. Indeed, for Deming, the statistical control of the variance, found in the products generated in the process of production, **is a way** to control the quality on the process **but it is not the heart** of the Excellence Deming advocates.

The confusion surrounding the concept of **Total Quality Management** is aggravated because terms such as Quality Management, Quality Control, Full Quality, Total Quality Control, Deployment of Quality Function and Program for Quality Improvement are used in books.

Sometimes, they are used as synonyms of Total Quality; other times they are not, contributing in this way to increase the difficulty to understand the TQM idea.

Therefore, I suggest that, whenever the term Quality appears in a text, the readers should not understand it as a synonym of Total Quality Management until they are sure about the meaning the author has given to the term Quality in this specific text.

Mainly, there are **three very different meanings** for the term "quality": Product Quality, Process Quality (or Quality Certification) and Total Quality or Excellence.

When the term Quality comes in a manual or in an article, the first thing to do is to try to understand which of these three meanings it is referring.

The Spanish Quality Association states that there are three different and successive stages regarding Quality:
- The Quality of **Products** and Services
- The Quality **Assurance** (or Quality Certification)
- Total Quality **Management** or **Excellence**

This Association underlines that there are three distinct and consecutive levels of Quality:
- Products and Services Quality Control
- Assuring the Quality Processes
- Total Quality

Quality Product is centered on defining **what** quality product or service is.

The idea of control appears associated to quality product. That is, as a tool to check, through inspections, if the product/service meets the pre-established specifications and to eliminate defective products.

The **Quality Assurance**, or Quality Certification, is a tool to help ensure that the **processes** are efficient and adequately designed to produce and deliver a concrete product or service, considering that if the production process of a given product or service has been well studied and defined, it must ensure that all products coming from this process are identical.

Total Quality Management is a philosophy, a culture, a strategy, a management style that enables and promotes the comprehensive and continuous quality improvement. Nowadays, it has become more customary to refer to TQM as Excellence Management, in order to avoid the confusion between TQM and Quality Certification, which has a different focus.

It is very important to understand that **these three approaches of Quality could exist separately.**

Therefore, there could be companies which produce **quality products** but do not have the Quality Certificate (of the process), for example the certification ISO 9000.

On the contrary, there may be companies that have the **Quality Certificate** but that produce inappropriate or unattractive products for the customers, because the product design is inadequate. Remember that an efficient production process does not change (does not redesign) the product but simply generates (produces) it according to the original design.

There may also be companies that implement **Total Quality Management** (TQM) but, at least initially, do not generate products or services without defects.

Let us keep in mind that the product quality is not achieved immediately after the adoption of the decision to implement Total Quality but once it is already established.

Quality products stem from a correct process of product **design**, a good definition of the **process** and its proper **execution**.

There are companies managed by the philosophy of Excellence or TQM Quality but that renounce to obtain the quality certificate ISO 9000 (for their processes).

That happens because, although this Certificate can reaffirm the image of the company and help to improve the processes, the company may have considered that the option for TQM is enough and that it does not want to incur in the costs involved in obtaining and maintaining the ISO 9000 Certificate in time.

8.2 Product Quality

Product, or Service, Quality is mainly linked to the product (or service) characteristics and to the customer perceptions.

Nevertheless, the product quality does not have a unique interpretation. What are we alluding to when we speak of the quality of a product?

Let us keep in mind that in some cases the idea of product quality is associated just with the product **price**; in other cases with its **scarcity** in the market; and sometimes with the technical **characteristics of the product**. All above gives room to understanding the concept of product quality as something difficult to define and manage.

In view of these thoughts, there may be those who say, *"Let us not be ambiguous. From the point of view of quality, the characteristics of the product are what really count".*

This statement, about what quality is, faces a complex reality: *What specific product features are we talking about?*

To answer this question the **standardization** of products appears. It defines the different characteristics of size, hardness, thickness, etc. which a product should have to be considered as first, second, third, etc. category.

However, is an orange classified as first category better than one classified as second category? Does a certain size or a certain color of an apple mean better flavor?

Does a wine with PDO (Protected Designation of Origin) have the same quality as another one with the same PDO? Does a wine with PDO from Rioja (a Spanish wine Region) better than another from Ribera del Duero (another Spanish wine region)? The consumer choices vary largely.

Ishikawa[16] gives an illustrative example that he personally experienced. He points out that for over two decades he studied the Japanese Industrial Norms referring to the in-roll paper for *newsprint*. These norms referred to the resistance, tension, and width of the roll, which are supposed to guarantee the quality of the paper.

However, a person in charge of Quality Control at a plant he visited told him: *"Sometimes we get complaints from printer houses in spite of the fact that the delivered product meets all the imperative industrial norms. Other times we do not get any complaints, although the product does not meet those norms. Therefore, we decided to ignore the Japanese industrial norms".*

Ishikawa asked him for more details and the person in charge of Quality Control explained *"the most frequent complaint is that the in-roll paper **breaks** during printing"*

With this example, Ishikawa wants to emphasize the **difficulty** that exists in many cases when we try **to define the parameters** that, if respected, guarantee product quality.

Customer satisfaction is essential when it comes to assessing the actual quality of the product but the producer often faces the difficulty of

---

[16] Kaoru Ishikawa (1915-1989). Professor and Chairman of Tokyo Musashi Institute

interpreting what the customer means by quality. For example, it is sometimes said that the customer *"wants the car to meet the requirement of being easy to drive"* but, **what does "easy drive ability" mean?** How can we measure this feature?

Product Quality is supposed to exist in the organizations that have introduced Total Quality Management, but these two concepts (Product Quality and TQM) are neither equivalent nor necessarily united. Quality articles can be produced by organizations not inspired by Total Quality. To put it in unequivocal terms: quality products could be even produced by organizations whose labor system is based on slavery!

Excellence in Management involves a collaborative, creative and dynamic approach to the management of all resources, human, material, technological and organizative. All this gives way to better processes, better products, more motivation and better results, including the development of people and their talents.

Implementing Excellence at an early stage does not necessarily mean achieving, from the very beginning, a high level of product quality **but it is a guarantee of success for the organization in the future** because its continuous approach to improvement will produce tangible and valuable results at a medium or even short-terms.

8.2.1 Quality from the client's point of view

From the point of view of the customer, there are three levels of quality: the expected quality, the satisfactory quality and the quality that delights.

The **expected quality** is achieved when the product or service has those features that customers take for granted and therefore do not explicitly ask for them when they require a particular service or product.

The citizen that requests an authorization from the Administration does not mention in his application that he wants a written reply with a legible writing, as he assumes that this will be so.

In a similar way, when a client is going to buy a new tire for his car, he expects that it will be homogenous and not pinched.

When the expected characteristics are given, the clients **agree** with it; when they are not given, the clients **are very discontent.**

Satisfying quality is achieved when the product or service includes **certain features** that customers **specifically** request. For example, when a client orders a steak well done or that the acquired tire be installed by 5.00 pm. When these requested features are offered, customers become satisfied; if not, they will be **dissatisfied**.

Finally, the **quality that delights** is achieved when the product or service includes characteristics the clients have not requested, because they did not think that they could have requested them or because they did not even imagine they existed.

We are talking about extraordinary characteristics added by the company. For example, serving the ordered steak on a specially decorated plate or giving the client when he pays for the bill a small advertising pen. When perks are given, the clients get **very satisfied; but if not, they do not become discontent**.

Then, what is the essence of quality? **What is the factor that most influences** the client's opinion about the quality of the purchased product or service?

To the complexity of the definition of the elements that constitute the quality of the product, we can add the fact that, for the clients, **quality does not remain limited to** whether the product or service really entails **the qualities it claims to have**.

The modern concept of quality emphasizes particularly **how the organization satisfies** its customers, **including** the way they are handled on the phone, how quickly the staff responds to a client's request, prepares a budget for him or responds to his complaints.

The Forum Corporation carried out researches on 14 very important industrial and services companies to learn the **reasons why some of their clients had left** those companies in the past year.

The results showed that:
a) 15% of the clients left because they had found a "*better product*" (with **less** flaws or with a lower flaw index)
b) 15% because they had found "*a **cheaper** product*"
c) 20% due to "*the **lack of contact** and personal attention*" from the previous provider and
d) 50% because the "***relations** with the provider's staff were of poor quality*".

Briefly:
a) Fifteen percent were lost due to the problems determined by the quality of the **product**.
b) Fifteen percent were lost due to the **price**.
c) **Seventy percent** left because they did not like the **relation** they had with the provider.

The conclusion is obvious: the client wants to obtain a product or service with certain characteristics but in the end, what influences his perception of quality most is **the relation with the providers**.

The client is ready, on many occasions, to excuse a flaw if the provider is efficient at listening to his request or complaint and makes an effort to correct any flaw.

It is obviously not possible to assess a product or service as a quality product when it has defects, but the client is probably not going to leave the company if the treatment received by the supplier shows an unwavering desire to serve and clear determination to repair the defects.

8.2.2 Quality from the point of view of the company

From the point of view of the producer, the term quality has another nuance. Quality for the company means to bring the activities of the organization to the position its manager wants it to play in the market.

The manager of a company or organization that operates in the market aims at economic success, and from this point of view, it is possible to say that the company operates with quality when it achieves economic success.

A company that views economic success, from the point of view of quality should:

1. **Offer attractive** products for its customers. That requires identifying the customers' needs and desires and developing products that meet those needs and requirements

2. Realize **profitable sales** which implies selling at prices above the costs

3. Maximize the benefits of their sales, **producing efficiently**, with minimum costs. That requires to:
   a) Be efficient at using resources: not wasting resources (human, technological, materials, alliances, etc).
   b) Produce through efficient processes and procedures that minimize or eliminate duplication or wastage
   c) Eliminate activities that do not add value to satisfy the needs of external customers or the organization.

In the case of the Public Administration, as well as of many other organizations (NGOs, political parties, etc.) whose results are not measured just by their economic profit, success is associated with the achievement of a good external image, the employee's satisfaction, the maintenance of a level of expenditure considered adequate to the number of services generated and so on.

Similarly to what happens in a business organization, quality in Public Administration is deemed to offering attractive services to the clients and a good image (which in the Administration is usually equivalent to profitable sales in the private sector) at a reasonable cost.

The queries to the client, the identification of their needs and the design of new services will allow the Public Administration to offer attractive services and, if the attention to the client is adequate, to achieve a good image.

However, how is it possible for the State to simultaneously achieve all this and have **reasonable costs**?

Here is where the main difficulties appear for those organizations that are not governed by the market and, therefore, cannot use the benefits indicator, an indicator that some consider questionable. Nevertheless it is, after all, a quantitative indicator. In the case of such organizations, the best way to analyze their "profitability" is to compare their results and costs with other similar organizations.

However, in the absence of such comparable data from other organizations, the alternative solution proposed by Total Quality Management is the promotion of an ongoing dialogue with the staff. The purpose of this dialogue is to find out, together with the staff, the phases of the processes that do not add value, in order to eliminate them.

The staff's suggestions are also very important for the creation of new products or services that could be useful for clients.

8.2.3 Simultaneous quality for the customer and the organization

One wonders whether it is feasible to match the customer's interests and those of the organization. Total Quality gives a definite answer: it is not only possible to satisfy both interests but to do so is **the most appropriate way** to ensure that the company or organization achieves success.

Indeed, to achieve success a company should follow the following principles:

a) The sales will be successful and will create a stable customers foundation only to the extent to which the **customers perceive** that the company offers quality both in the product itself and in the way of treatment and after-sale care.

b) The organization will be able to satisfy its customers only if it **identifies their needs** and meets or exceeds their expectations. Total Quality Management emphasizes that customer's opinions are an invaluable tool that helps to improve the product design to fit customer needs and offers information about the customers' perception of the treatment given by the company, allowing for actions of improvement.

c) The organization will be able to maximize its profit only if it manufactures products or services efficiently, with minimal costs. That requires producing under **efficient processes** that minimize rework or waste and eliminate those activities that are not oriented to meet the needs of external customers.

d) The organization will be able to improve the efficiency of processes if it requests **suggestions** from its employees, who know the production processes and are on the right position to discover opportunities for the improvement of the processes.

e) The quality of the relationship with the clients and the constructive contribution of suggestions from employees are only possible if they **feel integrated** and committed to the company.

Total Quality is not stingy with the level of quality of both the products and the attention given to the customer.

TQM motto is *"give the customers the highest level of quality allowed by the price of the product they pay for"*.

Moreover, Total Quality believes that **quality is the future.** The customer will be increasingly willing to pay more for what they consider quality products or services, rather than going after cheaper products and services of dubious quality.

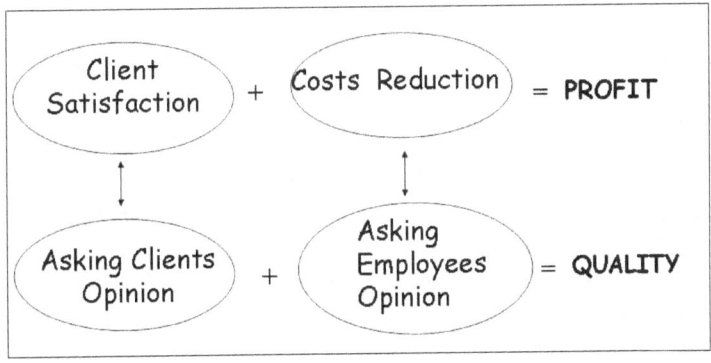

Total Quality Management advocates for the improvement of the **quality of the product as a strategic guideline**. Actually, many companies adopt this course of action and take advantage of the pull of its quality image, both to diversify its activities and to create brands, with different levels of product and service quality, covering a wider range of prices and qualities. **That allows them to reach other market segments.**

One example of this attitude is the Spanish company El Corte Ingles, a department store chain, which adopted as its brand both the product and the customer service quality. It has subsequently created Hipercor (hypermarket chain) with a range of lower-priced products, leveraging the brand image of quality that El Corte Inglés has; a chain of stores, Opencor, which is open 24 hours a day; Supercor, as a medium-sized neighborhood supermarket, etc...

The *"white label brands"* or *"unbranded products"* are another example of the use of a brand image quality. They were created by various supermarket chains, which initially **unmarked** packaged goods (without brands), often in **white** containers (hence its name).
Obviously, what these alimentation chains do is to offer the customers the implicit guarantee that the products have a certain level of quality **because** they were the ones **the chain selected** to sell.
The so-called *"white products"* evolved by acquiring the "brand name" that they really had (Auchan products, Hipercor products, Day products, Carrefour products, etc): that is, the brand of the alimentation chain that was selling them.

Indeed, nowadays, these distribution companies are very sensitive to the quality of the products they offer under their own brand, even more so than to the quality of the rest of products they sell, because they are aware that the reputation of its own brand is at stake.

If defective products are sold under their brands or if those companies were not attentive to the recommendations or to the customer's complaints regarding those products, they could significantly damage the image of quality they had obtained, and that would affect the entire line of business under its brand.

8.3 Process Quality

Everything works through processes. Giving birth, breathing, eating, the photosynthesis, etc. all are actions that follow more or less complex processes.

The same happens with any human activity, be it individual or corporative. Everything is done through processes: from frying an egg to solving a mathematics problem, going through manufacturing a chair.

However, as we can well imagine, it is not possible to solve any problem just because a process is being used, as, for example, in the above mentioned mathematics problem. As it is obvious, there can be steps to be followed in order to analyze and reflect on the mathematical problem but, where should we include the inspiration?

Consequently, it should be pointed out that there are no processes that guarantee the achievement of good results in the social, economic or political fields, as we can see in activities such as the enforcement of the law (justice) or governing a country or an organization.

Of course, defining processes that show what data is needed, how to collect it, what importance to attribute to it, etc. is helpful to enforce the law or to facilitate the leadership. However, neither justice nor leadership should be left in the hands of an automatic process.

Nevertheless, it is very useful to define the production processes in the industrial or services sectors.

So, it is possible to guarantee, to a great extent, that the items produced in this process be homogeneous and that the services (i.e transport) include some aspects that are essential (safety, speed, punctuality, cleanliness...)

Furthermore, the analysis of the process allows us to identify and eliminate steps of the process that are inefficient, be it because of the way they are performed, because they are redundant, because they may have been integrated together in a single phase or operation, or because they are performed by another employee, etc.

The need for a product to be a clear outcome of the requirements imposed by its design is much more urgent when it comes to products that should be **inevitably reliable** and work properly.

This urgency took place during World War II. It was imperative that the weapons and ammunition worked well and so the initiative to standardize the production procedures, which were then inspected by high-ranking army officials to verify that standards were met.

Once the war was over, the terms *"inspection"* and *"control"* began to be associated with quality. With this, it was ensured that the production met the specifications. So, later, quality was associated with *"conformance to specifications"*

In 1946, Delegates from 25 Countries met at the Institute of Civil Engineers in London and decided to create a new international organization *"to facilitate the international coordination and unification of industry standards"*

In February 1947 a new organization was created, ISO (International Organization for Standardization), based in Geneva, officially began its operations.

The standards developed by ISO are voluntary, as ISO is a nongovernmental organization. Therefore, it has no authority to impose its standards on any country. The content of the standards are protected by copyright and to access them individuals and businesses must purchase them.

In the USA, in the late 50's, a "Quality Program Requirements" was developed, and it produced a first quality standard which was applied in the military sector. Then, NASA promoted the development of the inspection of systems and processes to ensure quality. By 1962, criteria that suppliers have to meet in order to deal with entities such as NASA, were established.

In 1979, the BS 5750, a precursor to ISO 9000, was first published in the United Kingdom. It was a method whose aim was the control of production processes. Therefore, it was defined as a method of control.

In 1987, BS 5750 becomes ISO 9000 under the endorsement of the International Organization for Standardization,

The ISO 9000 norms are methodologies that indicate that any process, which has been designed in accordance with those norms, guarantees that the products or services resulting from the process adjust to the designed specifications, that is, to the characteristics that had been established initially as the desired correct ones (size, weight, strength, presentation, delivery place, etc.)

But a Quality Director of Motorola was categorical: *"with the ISO 9000 norms we can obtain very bad processes and products. Even a manufacturer of life vests made of cement can get the ISO 9000 certificate as long as these vests are produced in accordance with documented procedures and the company gives detailed instructions regarding the possible complaints about the flaws. This is absurd".* [17]

Among the various criticisms of the certification process there are the following:
a) The amount of money, time and paperwork required for certification.
b) It states that there is specification, control and procedures but not quality product improvement.
c) It is valid as a **guide** from which to learn. However, it does not guarantee the quality of a **product** but only that it has been produced following a predetermined process.
d) It is noted that many companies only seek to obtain the certificate but not to apply the procedures.

On the other hand, the opinions of key TQM gurus are very important.
Philip B. Crosby stated: *"All techniques for quality control are pointless if the management staff does not have a well-defined objective. There is no need to spend time and money on systems such as ISO 9000 and Baldrige. Quality is not obtained from*

---

[17] Nevertheless, at present Motorola itself has a ISO 9000 certificate due to the image effect it has worldwide.

reading books, although they may serve **as a guide**. Quality derives from a good management"

Joseph M. Juran, in an exclusive interview published in Quality Digest in 1998 expressed some of his thoughts about the standards for quality management to answer to the Quality Digest question: *What is your opinion about the series of quality management standards ISO 9000 and its derivatives?*

His answer was:

"The basic concept has some merit in itself. Companies like to know about their ability to produce good results. This set of standards has outlined a number of things that a company should be doing. Many companies have decided that they cannot get into a situation where their competitor is certified and they are not. That is a marketing disadvantage. The criterion for certification has some pretty useful elements"

From my point of view, to have a certification ISO 9000 does not guarantee that a company will become a quality leader. There is no proof. We do not have any research that states that those companies which are certified according to ISO 9000 have products with a higher quality than those produced by companies that are not certified. I have seen some research comparing products that have come from certified companies and products that have come from non-certified companies, and the authors found no difference"

"That has never been properly studied and, until it is, we have no reason to conclude that ISO 9000 certification produces better results.

In fact, when you look at companies that have achieved leadership in quality, you can find out that some things they did -training the management on how to manage quality, the achievement of improvements year after year, securing the participation of the work-force- are not present in ISO standards 9000. In my opinion, if one adheres to the ISO 9000 and not develops it further, then it is almost possible to say that he will not be leader in quality, because one would be obviating vital ingredients"

In short, in many cases the lack of quality of a product can be due to the fact that the production process was not successfully completed. Total Quality involves aspects that go far beyond the certification process and venture into the field of Management.

8.4 Total Quality Management.

In 1950, the Association of Japanese Scientists and Engineers invited the American Edwards Deming to deliver several conferences whose essential purpose was to help to improve the quality of Japanese products -quite poor at that time.

Deming's message was sharp and clear: the defects that arise in the production processes can be largely reduced if the processes are controlled, analyzed and reviewed.

This is the only effective way to ensure the quality of the production processes. **However, to achieve this**, it is necessary that the employees be are motivated to monitor and review the processes, to identify their weaknesses and propose improvements. That also applies to any type of processes: production, support, strategic,

The management philosophy advocated by Deming, Total Quality Management, became very popular in Japan because it fit well with the Japanese culture and mentality.

In Japan, the traditional culture, with deep roots in Confucianism and Buddhism, gives priority to group versus individual. Hence, the process of creativity and decision-making takes place in a context of a large group interaction. The initiatives are formulated and presented on behalf of the group, rather than the individual, as it happens in the West. That facilitates cooperation and transparency.

The Japanese culture was an excellent breeding ground for the TQM philosophy as

Deming's suggestions attach **great importance to the cooperative relations**.

The development and competitiveness of Japanese industry surprised the West and pushed the U.S. companies to discover and learn the *"secrets"* of Japanese management.

So, the ideas of the fellow American Deming, that had found a fertile ground in Japan in the 50's, began in the 80's -**thirty years later**- to be welcomed in the US, the country where he had been born **and where he still lived** Once more the phrase *"no one is a prophet in one's own land"* was proving true.

Besides Deming, the main theoreticians of Total Quality today were Crosby[18], Juran[19] and Ishikawa.

In Europe, Total Quality has penetrated deeply, from the late 80s on.

As a result, on 19th October 1989, fourteen key European enterprises, created the **European Foundation for Quality Management**.

---

[18] Phillip Crosby (1926-2001). Businessman, consultant and author who contributed to management theory and quality management practices

[19] Joseph Juran (1904-2008). Engineer and consultant. He worked in Japan to introduce the quality approach

This Foundation developed, based on the precedent Japanese and American models, a methodology, the European Model of Excellence, whose purpose is to help leaders to check if their organizations are functioning properly in accordance with the principles of Total Quality Management.

The model advocates self-assessment, which is meant to help managers to identify **where**, in **what** aspects of the organization and to **which** degree, **it is necessary to implement** or reinforce the key pillars of an Excellent Management.

8.4.1 Clarifying what Total Quality is

Rafael Aguayo's book, *"The Deming's method"*, using the ideas of his teacher Dr. Deming, contains reflections and points of view which clarify what **Total Quality Management** is.

These ideas help to overcome the confusion that often exists regarding the term Quality and its implications.

The traditional idea of quality is often associated with the existence of a Department of Quality Control that reviews the products to rule out those with defects. In this way it tries to ensure that only a very small percentage of those products, which reaches the consumer, are defective. This idea of quality control has very little to do with the type of management proposed by the philosophy of Total Quality.

Deming believes, according to Aguayo, that *"quality control means knowledge, particularly knowledge of variation and processes, training and lifelong learning and **enthusiasm** for the work"*.

In short, when Deming uses the concept "quality control" he does not refer to the statistical analysis of the results of the processes **but to the knowledge** of why the variation takes place. This knowledge is obtained through the intensive **cooperation** between employees and managers when revising the processes, identifying the problems and suggesting actions to correct them hereinafter.

To further emphasize the difference between Total Quality Management and the inspection of product quality, Aguayo reminds us that Deming proposes a surprising recipe: *"Stop relying on mass inspection to achieve quality"*.
Deming does not advocate the total elimination of the inspection but says *"the inspection does not detect the problems inherent in the system."*
Indeed, Deming considers that it is a mistake to believe that quality improves when an inspector detects and rejects defective products. What he is improving is the likelihood of consumers buying

products without any flaws. It is even possible to assure that all the products offered for sale have no flaws, as it is the case if a 100% of the products are inspected. **Nevertheless, that does not improve the quality of the production system**.

If an inspection system is established -by sampling- to control the products produced by the employees, all that this inspection will ensure is that the percentage of defects in products for sales will not exceed a certain level.

However, the causes of manufacturing defects will remain unknown and therefore they will not be rectified.

If the process is not revised, there will always be a percentage of defective products. They will be eliminated (or reduced) by the traditional inspection but the cost of the inspection itself will obviously affect the price that is paid by the consumer, and besides, the production processes will not be improved.

In the same line Ishikawa states in his book *"What is Total Quality Control?"*:

"Inspectors are unnecessary personnel that reduce the overall productivity of the company. They do not manufacture anything. Inspection is necessary only because there are defects and defective items. If these disappear, inspectors would be unnecessary"

Deming advocated that the processes be always supervised, yet, not necessarily by inspectors but by those who have produced the product or service, that is to say, the employees themselves.

Elaborating on the topic, Aguayo says that in 1996 Dr. Joseph Juran, one of the quality gurus, wrote in the journal Industrial Quality Control: *"In Czechoslovakia there is the unfounded assumption that most of the failures are controllable by the operator, and that if workers show interest, quality problems in the factories would be significantly reduced"*.

This sentence points out to a very common point of view among many managers who consider that the cause of the defects is mainly the employees.

This assumption which holds the intention to improve quality, leads to the increase of the control of the processes, monitoring closely what the workers do and enhancing products inspection.

However, Deming, Juran and Ishikawa make it very clear **that this is not the point of Total Quality Management**.

Deming emphasizes that 94 % of failures are attributable to the system and not to the employee. Juran reduces the rate slightly to 80%.

Something similar happens with Ishikawa who states that when a plant produces defective items or fails at something, only 20 to 25% of the blame can be attributed to line operators. The rest, 75-80%, is due to the system.

So the main TQM gurus conclude that between 75-94% of failures are attributable to the system. Only between 6-25% are attributable to the employee.

Deming also notes that the emphasis traditionally placed on the inspection or control has led to attitudes that are ultimately counterproductive for quality.

For example, he states that it is a serious error to increase the inspector's remuneration depending on the number of detected defective products. The more bugs they find, the greater their remuneration is. That, unfortunately, can induce them to report allegedly petty defective aspects of products that are not significant.

In such a context, the inspectors' real purpose would not be to improve quality but to improve their own remuneration. Deming considers it harmful when there are situations in which the interests of the company and the interests of the workers are confronted because this will be detrimental to the quality.

In the same line of giving emphasis to the importance of the inspection, **another common error** is to establish systems in which each step of the process is inspected two or more times.

When two individuals are doing, or revising, the same thing, which could be perfectly done by either of them, they will not really feel responsible for the task. The problem is that each tends to consider the other one either as his substitute or as an inspector.

In administrative bureaucracy the bosses often sign in acknowledgement of the work that has been done by his subordinates, merely because of their hierarchical position. That leads to a number of **signatures in chain**. In these cases, the signatures often have no other purpose than to show the command line **without actually contributing** to a substantial review of the decision or proposal made.

When an employee is considered just as a part of a machine that performs a certain process, it is difficult to make him feel responsible for what he does. In this case, even when the employee is threatened with sanctions if he makes mistakes, this still will not lead to the improvement of his performance.

The inspection, centered on the product sampling analysis, admits that there will always be a percentage, however small, of defective products that have escaped the eye of the inspection.

That is not the spirit of TQM, **which aims** at revising and amending the processes in such a way that, by themselves, they become capable of achieving zero defects.

The spirit of true quality is reflected in an anecdote that happened to a Japanese company when it began to work in the U.S. market for the first time. One American buyer ordered 50,000 units with the condition that there should be no more than three defective units for each 10,000.

When the American buyer received the shipment there was a letter from the Japanese company explaining that they were not familiar with American business methods and that it had taken them several days to figure out what it meant that *"the order should have no more than three defective pieces per 10,000 units".* They went on explaining that along with the 50,000 perfect units they had shipped 15 defective units, in a separate package, for the buyer to do with them whatever he wished.

When a process generates defects, steadily and significantly, due to the inaccuracy of the equipment used or the variability of the raw material, **what needs to be done is to include the inspection** of the product on the process itself, as another phase of the process.

Where a 100% inspection is applied, the inspection shall not be considered a monitoring process but another phase of the process itself.

Indeed, Deming recommends a 100 % inspection in cases where the nature or circumstances of the process do not ensure the absence of errors.

When it is absolutely necessary, for safety reasons, to ensure that the pieces produced have no defects (for example, in a spatial vessel) the inspection of each of the pieces produced **must be included along the production process itself**.

On the contrary, Deming suggested that there is no need for inspection whatsoever when the process guarantees a very small defect level and when the defects will not cause important problems to the customer.

Total Quality promotes the idea that the organization **should focus on studying the causes** of defaults **to correct them at source**. So the final inspection can be eliminated.

In short, one of the TQM goals is to define processes in which both the **control** of raw materials and pieces used and the **design** of operations performed, ensure that the products obtained are identical. Therefore, no external inspection will be needed to ensure quality.

Nevertheless, Ishikawa underlines that the spirit of Total Quality should reject triumphalism and claims that *"those who think that under a uniform process the effects are always uniform are wrong. We will always have defective products."*

By this, he means that although it is assumed, in theory, that a robotic process will generate identical products to the original design, it is always necessary to perform some monitoring of results in order to correct unforeseen circumstances and adapt processes to possible variations in the raw materials, technologies, coordination operations between upstream and downstream, etc.

Quality products are not produced only by organizations that have adopted a system of Total Quality Management. Under other management philosophies quality products may also be produced.

However, all organizations that have adopted and implemented a Total Quality Management system **must** inexcusably produce quality products and **must** be innovative and creative organizations. If that does not happen, they should check whether they have implemented TQM correctly.

Total Quality requires a change in the traditional philosophy of management of all the company employees, especially the managers. TQM implies the adoption of a **new management philosophy**.

Manifesting the will to improve the quality of products and services do not imply that Total Quality philosophy has been implemented. It is a mere statement of will, which requires, above all, understanding what we want to do. Indeed, **there**

are many misconceptions about what implementing Total Quality Management in the organization means.

Aguayo said that observers only see what they have been trained to see and, with humor, he adds: *"when some American observers traveled to the East to discover the secrets of the Japanese management, they returned disappointed, because the only difference they found was the Japanese hobby for singing in the morning".* (He refers to the habit many Japanese companies have to make their employees sing the company or national anthem before going to work)

8.4.2 What Total Quality is not

One of the best ways to capture the essence of a particular philosophy is to understand its basic concepts, especially the ones different to those advocated by their opponents. Thus, the white color can be best understood as opposed to black.

In the following paragraphs, we will use the same method: to present the philosophy behind Total Quality as opposed to other frequent opinions. Indeed, **Excellence does not share some usual and common ideas** considered as the most appropriate ways to manage organizations.

1. *"Introducing Total Quality implies an additional cost to run the organization."* This statement is **incorrect.** It falls within the line of thought that believes that any process that adds value implies an additional cost and therefore a cut in benefits of the organization. Not so: Total Quality asserts that although the introduction of this management philosophy will initially lead to additional costs, they will be small and, besides, in the short run, these costs will be compensated for improved benefits.

2. *"A sufficient level of quality must be achieved to meet customer expectations"* This statement reflects a **narrow-minded** view of TQM concept. It is equivalent to say, *"Let us give the customers the minimum level of quality, **only enough** to satisfy them"*

This attitude does not induce the company to continuous improvement and frequently the company ends up losing part of its market share to other competitors that have not put ceiling to their product quality but have constantly made improvements beyond customers' expectations, attracting in this way their competitor's clients.

The company that truly believes in Total Quality considers quality as its brand image and is **always willing to seek further improvements**.

This attitude does not imply lack of rationality. It does not forget the production direct and indirect costs. It is evident that it would be ruinous to offer products whose prices were below their production costs. If the company believes in quality, it takes care of the price-cost ratio when trying to introduce improvements, and obviously rejects those improvements whose introduction involves a production cost higher than the price accepted at the market.

However, the cost should not lead a TQM organization to discard, a priori, the search for new improvements, among other things, because many of these improvements could be so appealing to the customer that would allow for higher prices.

3. *"The supervision is a key factor to improve quality"* TQM, without denying the fundamental role of the manager, believes that **his essential role is not to control the details** or to set up middle managers just to monitor the various stages of production.

TQM believes that if we design a proper process, the process itself will guarantee the quality of the product without having to rely on the watchful eye of a supervisor. The adage *"the eye of the master fattens the horse"* is not part of the philosophy of TQM. This would say, *"even if the master is not there, when TQM inspires the processes and the organization, the horse will gain weight"*

4. *"We have the responsibility to encourage workers; to empower them".* That sounds great, very modern, very updated. Tom Peters and many other authors have proposed to do so but the reality is that, in general, the workers are not granted autonomy to propose reforms for improvement. The workers are not really empowered. **No real empowerment is given to them.**

Quite often, there are no mechanisms through which to collect the employees' suggestions. Sometimes some innovative companies put the usual mailbox to collect suggestions from its employees but if the management style does not change, if it does not involve workers, most likely the mailboxes will remain empty.

Something similar happens when companies establish a system to reward the suggestions received. It works for a short time and then it is forgotten. Why is it so? Because only rewarding is not enough to promote a change in the culture of the company.

If the employees' participation is not constantly encouraged by the leadership, the empowerment will not work.

5. *"Workers' carelessness, bad will, lack of abilities or skills are the main causes of defects or faults in the product or service quality."* **TQM fully disagrees with this point of view.**

TQM considers that the processes and the organizational models themselves are the ones that generate workers' carelessness, bad will and lack of capacity or skill.

If an employee who is found idle is called to type the phone book list, so that he does not remain idle, he will then take note of that and will try not to be found idle in the future. Ordering him to type the phone book list (which is already on the computers or intranet) will not improve his cooperative attitude because he will find this order nonsense or a punishment. Giving him this type of order will probably stimulate his cunning to avoid, hereinafter, being caught in a "lazy" attitude. The alternative behavior TQM proposes consists **in giving the employee real opportunities** to put in action his talent.

6. *"Competition should be encouraged among the workers."* There is nothing wrong with motivating employees to improve their performance, taking as reference, the achievements of their peers. On the contrary, it is highly desirable to encourage them to improve the quality of products and processes.

However, **if the rules** regarding what we mean by competition **are not agreed and clarified**, there is a **grave risk** of creating very **damaging confrontations** in the organization.

In plain words: In these circumstances it is highly likely that some employees feel prone to hide their know-how, ideas and performances from their peers and to give importance only to the goals assigned to them, without worrying about the interests of the whole and even acting in detriment of others, if that seems convenient to their own interest.

7. *"The processes and organizational models can only be optimized by external experts and consultants."* This is an updated version of Taylor's approach: someone **from outside** the company designs processes and sets up what everyone must produce. This attitude has a major drawback: the **employees will not perceive the process as their own** but as something imposed on them. Consequently, they are neither motivated to improve the processes nor to give suggestions.

TQM, without denying the value of a good external advice or consultancy, considers that *"Those who know better both the technical and organizational details of the processes of an organization are the employees themselves. They are the ones who know where the problems lie and have ideas on how to correct them."*

8. *"The key for progress and improvement is the introduction of new technologies, computers and robotics".* Obviously, these techniques allow the processes to run faster and more accurately and to offer richer information. That is, they make the processes faster and more efficient and self-controlled. However, who designs, reviews and improves the processes? A flawed process, if robotic, runs faster than before, but it still is a flawed process. So the **key point resides on a good process design.**

9. *"Assigning production goals and performance standards to the workers is the best way to increase productivity".* This has the disadvantage that workers focus only on meeting the quotas imposed on them but they do not worry about the final quality of the resulting product or about the costs incurred to achieve the quotas that the management has imposed.

Does it mean that TQM is against goals and quotas? The answer is emphatic: **No**. What TQM questions is: *"Who and how is setting the goals and quotas?"* That is really the Gordian knot of the success or failure of the productive system. **Using a participatory process** for setting goals and quotas is a condition for success. This is the point of view of the TQM philosophy.

10. *"The method of carrot and stick is the most effective way to lead and motivate the employees".* Admittedly, fear induces to action, but in which direction? Which degree of loyalty is expected?

TQM emphasizes that it is essential, even more in today's complex processes, to rely on the responsibility of the workers to some extent. It is not profitable to place a supervisor behind each worker. **The best way is to create a climate of shared responsibility.**

Nevertheless, it is necessary to differentiate between content and form, between creating fear and speaking in a tone of mild or delicate voice.

In some cases, a soft voice may conceal a worrying threat, while in other cases shouting may be natural in the process. Let us think of military maneuvers, construction works or other activities where the processes usually involve embedded instructions formulated by shouting. In these contexts, it is considered normal and therefore not threatening.

11. *"It is appropriate to reward the best performers. It is essential to introduce the assessment by merit and payment of incentives"* It is natural that responsibility, initiative and special efforts have correlation with the payment -of all kinds- that a person may receive.

However, we should be aware that in many areas of activity it is not easy to assess and identify each person's merits because there are no set of standards of what is a proper productivity per person.

That is why the merit criterions are often defined from above and then applied with no further considerations. It may happen that what at first sounded like **a wonderful idea (evaluating the merits) becomes a source of tension,**

rivalry and difficulties for cooperation. TQM do not support the merit assessment and payment of incentives, **unless the members of the organization agree the rules**.

12. *"The key point is that the final product or service meets the design specifications"* Obviously, there is nothing wrong with this rule.

The problem may lie **in how the design was elaborated**: Have you consulted the clients? Have you consulted the workers? Do the workers know what value each of the product specifications aims to provide? Were the workers consulted about whether there is a better way to achieve this?

If these consultations were not done, the organization would probably have lost, first, the opportunity to receive valuable suggestions and, second, the opportunity to make the employees feel the product as their own.

As we can see, TQM questions the value of these twelve traditional corporate *"recipes"* and points out that, even when applying them with the best of intentions, they may lead the organization to failure or poor results, if all the implications of these *"management recipes"* are not adequately understood.

The criticisms made, on TQM's behalf, to these traditional recipes, could lead the readers to conclude that Total Quality is nothing but a management technique centered on promoting consensus, participation and human relations. **This conclusion would be erroneous and incomplete**.

Human Resources participation is a key and important aspect of Total Quality Management. However, there are other factors which are essential (**goals, processes, results**) and that should be included in the whole approach of TQM.

8.4.3 Definitions of Total Quality Management

Important leading organizations in the business world have formulated definitions of what they mean by quality. In many cases, they do not precise accurately what the quality contents are. In others, the definition is limited to the Product or Process quality but does not define Total Quality.

Here are some of them:
- *Continued pursuit of perfection by the company as a whole* (Sieger LTD). This definition includes the idea of **continuous** improvement but requires explaining what perfection means. We should remember that what was perfect management for Taylor, was not perfect management for Tom Peters or Munsterberg.

- *Searching for excellence and customer's satisfaction.* (Texas Instruments Ltd) As in the previous case, it includes the word of excellence, which needs to be defined as well.

- *Quality unites all in a chain of efforts to achieve customer's satisfaction* (Cooper Burto Brewery). It emphasizes the **unity** of all to achieve customer's satisfaction, although it does not precise how it is going to be achieved.

- *Quality means total customer's satisfaction* (RHP Bearings). This definition fits the concept Quality **Product** but neither the Quality Process nor the Total Quality. As it was already indicated, a product may give satisfaction to customers even when it has been produced in a system of forced labor, and that is not a Total Quality Management system.

- *Quality means that products and services meet the exact requirements of customers* (Cossor Electronics). It is similar to the previous definition, centered on **Product** Quality.

- *Products and services that fully meet internal and external customers' requirements, from the beginning, in time, and always* (ICL). It includes the aspects of the customer's satisfaction and the employee's (internal customer) satisfaction. Anyway, it does not clarify how it intends to provide that satisfaction.

We propose the following **definition**:
*"Total Quality Management or Excellence Management is a system that has as its central principle, a **permanent attitude of improving** products and services, as well as processes, aimed at meeting the needs of clients in a fair return for what they directly, via prices or rates, or indirectly (taxes) paid for them.*
*The main TQM tools are the collection **and** the **analysis of** suggestions from customers and employees, in order to improve the **design** of products and services. Also TQM collects and analyses the employees' suggestions to improve production **processes and functioning** of the organization"*

Excellence implies, above all, an attitude to **adapt products and services** to customer's desires and needs, both present and future, which will produce good results in profits and/or image.

The experience shows that the **employee's attitude** is a key factor to achieve both customer's satisfaction and continuous process improvement. It is the employee who detects, in their day to day, multiple small suggestions or requests from the clients, and who in his job position, discovers possible ways to simplify and make the **processes** more productive.

Similarly, it is very intelligent to consider the **customer as a valuable contributor** to the company. With their complaints and suggestions, the company receives orientation to detect the defects and improve its products and services.

Why use the name of Total Quality? The use of the adjective "**TOTAL**" means that the TQM includes:

a) **Product or service quality** in **its fullest sense**: It includes not only the product or service itself but also the packaging, the delivery date, the invoice clarity, the customer treatment, the reception and answer of complaints and suggestions, etc.

b) The constant revision and improvement of the **quality of all the Processes**, such as the process of product design, manufacturing process, process control of raw materials and parts, the process of measuring and evaluating products, the billing process, the process for handling complaints and suggestions, etc.

c) The **quality of the Management system**. It requires a style able to involve the efforts and interests **of all** participants: managers, employees, customers, suppliers and all stakeholders.

In short, TQM wants to emphasize that Total Quality, **as a management system**, means that Quality must inspire all and every one of the actions of the organization in order that all parties involved (customers, employees, suppliers, stakeholders, etc.) consider that their interrelationships must really be an example of quality and contribute to improve quality.

9 THE FOUR PILLARS

Most modern organizations foresee ways or measures with which to correct the errors that may happen.

Still, many of these measures are not successful because:

a. **Usually**, they **are not preventive measures**, but are designed and applied once the problems have arisen and, what is worse, many times just with the intention of finding who to blame.
b. They neither **include mechanisms meant to collect** the problems that the workers confront daily nor their possible **suggestions**.

Within the complex and specialized modern organizations, an efficient **improvement system** needs to:

- Establish mechanisms meant to **identify** the problems that arise or may arise.
- Make possible the **participation** of the people that intervene in these processes to suggest possible corrective measures.
- **Communicate** these proposed measures to the whole company in case there are alternative suggestions.

- Make it clear that **the management level** will **support** the suggested measures, once agreed.

Total Quality acts on that line. It is not just a well-intentioned declaration of principles. It implies a clear and systematic management that relies on the following four pillars: **clients/customers, human resources, process and a continuous improvement spirit**.

If any of these four pillars is not used properly, it is not possible to say that the organization applies Total Quality Management principles. It may be looking for Quality Product or to obtain a Quality Process Certificate (ISO 9000 or others), but with this only, the organization would not be operating under the philosophy of Total Quality.

9.1 External clients

From the quality point of view, a client is any person or entity that receives the products or services elaborated at a working place or by a productive unit.

The concept of client is not applied exclusively to somebody that buys a product on the market.

A client is also every citizen who comes to the **Public Administration** in demand of a particular service, even if it is required by law to do so (e.g. to make the Declaration of Income Tax).

Regarding the citizen as a client creates psychologically a different relation, as he is no longer considered as being *"someone who is begging for an act of generosity"* from the Civil Servants, but as someone who *"buys a service"* that the Administration provides.

Therefore, he has the right to show his discontentment with regard to the service received. The term *"client",* in the public sphere, invites the Public Administration to have the mindset of offering special treatment and having the concern for serving every client.

In the private sphere, where the benefit of the company depends on the achievement and maintenance of a market share, the interest in the client is even more rooted.

The importance of **fostering client loyalty** is increasingly bigger. That is, it is becoming more and more important that the client buy again in our company, because he perceives it as a company that produces quality products, is interested in improving them and tries to offer the client the highest satisfaction.

Total Quality defines **External Clients** as those people or entities that **acquire the final** products or services of a company or institution.

As the name indicates, the External Clients are people or entities that **are outside** the organization that offers products or services.

One of the first tasks of every organization that wants to implement TQM philosophy is **to identify its clients/customers**, answering the following questions:
- How many **types** of clients do I have?
- Which is the most numerous **group**?
- What is the **importance** of each group for the organization?
- What **products or services** is every one of them using and to what extent?

It is possible to summarize the activity of a company or organization through the identification and quantification of its clients and the products it offers them.

Once this simple radiography of the organization is prepared, Total Quality signals that the company must **know its clients' opinions in detail**:
- What products satisfy them and why?
- What faults have they found in different products?
- How does the company treat them?
- What suggestions do they make to improve the product or the service?

This information is very valuable for the organization as, although it does not represent the only decision-making source, it designates the horizon that the organization must head to. Let us remember the difficulties we previously underlined to define the essence of product quality in few objective parameters.

That is the reason why **the client is a valuable source of information** to orient the company towards defining more precisely the idea and characteristics of a product quality.

Total Quality shows that **we must stop considering clients' complaints as a problem.** On the contrary, their complaints are information that the client gives freely.

We must not hinder this process in any way; we cannot treat the clients who are filing a complaint in a rude manner. We must see them as people who are using their time to communicate freely about something they consider a fault.

Ishikawa asks the following question: *'Why are there so many difficulties to discover the faults in the products that end in the consumer's hands?*

His answer is:
"**First of all**, *consumers are not used to make detailed complaints. Maybe they would, if they found a fault in an expensive item, but usually nothing is said about most items. As a result, their dissatisfaction remains unknown.*

Then, they just choose another brand when they go back for a similar product. That is why it is very important to obtain information through the complaints. So, consumers must be encouraged to write down complaints.

Secondly, *the information obtained about through complaints from users and consumers* **disappears** *along the way and never reaches the manufacturing company that produced the item".*

Total Quality emphasizes that to make it easy for the clients to file complaints and, especially, suggestions, has a double advantage:
- a) On one hand, it fosters the **client's loyalty** to the company, because they understand that the manufacturing company is listening to them

b) On the other hand, it is a rich **source of information** and suggestions.

Obviously, the moment these facilities are provided, the number of complaints will rise, at least in a first phase, but **this must not discourage** the company. On the contrary, as Ishikawa says: "*the rise of the number of complaints is a clear signal of the efficiency of the system to collect complaints and suggestions created by the company*".

Unfortunately, **in most companies, the reality is just the opposite**: the complaint filed by a client is seen as something bad, that we must get rid of as fast as we can, instead of being considered as free and valuable information that can detect and help to correct the errors committed by the company.

9.2 Internal Clients

During the industrial development, the concept of enterprise was based mainly on the idea of investment, the idea of **industrial** or **financial capital**.

In the modern era, enterprises have realized that a very important part of the enterprise value is based on the knowledge or abilities of their staff, the management and the technical or organizational levels.

In the services sector, many enterprises (training, consultancy, legal assistance, etc) have very few material or financial means. Its main factors are the expertise, the knowledge, and the abilities that reside on their human resources.

Human resources have started to be called the **Human capital** of the organization. In this line, **Excellence attributes a primordial importance** to the human resources of the organization. To emphasize its importance, Excellence considers the employees as **the Internal Clients** of the organization.

Ishikawa reports that an executive director of CBS/Sony once told him: *"We have many visitors from Europe and the United States that want to see the technology we use to produce phonographic records. They know that our records sound better, but when they visit the factory, they discover we are working with the same technology, the same press and the same raw material. Some of them insist upon the fact that we have secret solutions and ask us to let them inspect our waste. They, of course, find nothing different from their waste. They are so disoriented when I tell them that the sound quality* **difference does not lie in our machines, but in our people***"*.

Raw material, machines and processes are very important in the manufacturing process, but they depend on the operation by the employees, even in the case of highly automated processes. Therefore, we can say that the employees' knowledge, their attitude and their interest in the work, largely influence the results of the enterprise.

The type of relation that the organization maintains and cultivates **with its employees has a great impact** on their actions, on their motivation, on the results and even on the development of the enterprise know-how.

Total Quality Management chooses to emphasize the importance of the employees. That is why it calls them Internal Clients, intending to say that human resources are not a mere resource that the organization manages, but must be considered as a **pool of clients who the organization must pay attention to.** Otherwise, it might risk losing them or, at least, losing their talents.

Every job position, or production unit, can be perceived, on one hand, as a **Provider** and, on the other hand, as a **Client**.

Every job position or production unit has give and take actions with its environment. Thus, an employee can **receive** instructions from his superior and, **in exchange,** create a product or service (for example, doing a technical report, filling out a questionnaire, archiving a file, a resolution proposal, etc.) and **provide** it to his boss or to the unit that requested it.

In fact, when the boss requests an employee to do something, what he is actually doing is similar to what the clients of any organization do when they request a certain product or service from it.

In this case, the boss is the Client of the employee, although his request is based on the hierarchical authority he holds. That is why the employee must satisfy this *"Client"* (his boss), whose first responsibility is to **clearly formulate his "orders"**, that is, to give clear instructions to the employee in regard to what he is asking for.

Just like the clients pay the sellers for the products and services they buy at the market, the boss, in a company, **remunerates (pays) the "provider" (the employee) through the salary** and through the perspectives of promotion, professional recognition, personal relations, etc.

We can say, in a reciprocal way, that the **employee is also a "Client"** of his boss to the extent that he "buys" or does not buy (assumes or rejects) his boss's orders, management style or organizational philosophy, and actions geared to motivate him, etc.

The boss, in his position of "provider", should care for the employee ("client") **asking him how he, the boss, could improve** the "product" (instructions, philosophy, motivation capacity, etc.) that gives continuously to the employee.

The boss must not be just a boss, but a **coordinator** that promotes improvement of the organization.

Seeking the employee's opinion, with intelligence, appropriate techniques and at the right time does not mean that the boss is giving up his leadership position.

On the contrary, **he is creating a context of trust** with the employee that will allow him (the boss) to know the employee's opinions and suggestions. Later, when the manager (the boss) considers appropriate, he will adapt his leadership style to the one more adequate for his internal clients (employees) and for the organization.

Total Quality Management highlights the idea that human resources should be seen as **Internal Clients**. All working positions are, at a certain extent, Internal Clients of other positions within the organization. Thus, every unit or employee is also the client of those units or employees that provide them with office materials, a computer list, juridical or technical counseling, reports, etc.

Excellence points out that calling the employee by the name "internal client" will undoubtedly help to overcome the traditional tendency to consider the employee a mere subordinate whose unique mission is to obey his superiors' orders.

The concept of "internal client" emphasizes, by analogy with the external client, the need to treat the employee as a "client" who we want to sell our "product", that is, our wish that he, the employee, involves himself in making the company better and more productive. It may sounds utopic but Excellence has proven that it is absolutely possible.

Therefore**, a frequent error** is to consider that the employee's suggestions must be **strictly limited to improving the production processes** and that they must not interfere, not even by making suggestions, in management and, even less, in organizational issues.

Total Quality believes that we must **not rule out the idea** that the employees can make suggestions for the improvement of any aspect of the organization, such as processes, products or services, and even, for the organizational structure and functioning norms (distribution of competences, communication problems, incentive systems, etc.)

A solid company must not fear that its employees discuss constructively the hierarchical structure, the professional promotion system and even the remuneration system. On the contrary, it is convenient to stimulate all forms of suggestions.

The employees' common sense, their educational level and their available time will allow them to focus on formulating suggestions in the domains in which they feel they are best prepared. Obviously, the case of an employee at a lower level formulating proposals for the reorganization of the company is less frequent.

The manager should consider any employee suggestion, regarding the products or the modification of the form of management, as a **proof of the employee's interest** in the company.

Of course, all employees' suggestions (proposals) **must be accompanied by a justification** explaining why they consider that their suggestion will add value to the current production of the organization and what the additional cost implied by the implementation of their suggestions might be.

9.2.1 Disparity between Managers and Employees' opinions

Unfortunately, most companies or organizations are often not interested in obtaining the opinion of the staff and even try to avoid it, missing in this way an enormous potential of precious suggestions.

When companies conduct surveys among the employees, in a context that guarantees total anonymity, the results of the surveys often show that the organizations have been underusing its employee's talents and capacities.

A gap between the managers and the employees that prevents real and fluid communication manifests that the organization is not using employees' potential at the due level.

As an example, we are going to present the results of the survey the author of this book carried out, ensuring the anonymity of respondents.

These inquiries were conducted, in the nineties, among **eleven groups** of civil servants in the Spanish Public Administration.

Five of these groups were composed by participants that belonged to five different Government Departments (State Secretaries). The other six groups were mixed, having participants from several different Departments.

In the inquiries, all the participants in the eleven groups were asked the same questions.

First, the employees were asked **to choose 5 principles, out of a series of 22 that** they understood were a **priority for** their respective bosses.

Then, to quantify the importance given to each of those 5 principles, they should give 5 points to the one they considered **was most important to their boss**, 4 points to the second most important, 3 to the third, 2 to the fourth and 1 point to the one that was the least important to their boss.

After carrying out these inquiries, they were asked to fill the questionnaire out again, but this time on the hypothesis that they, each of them, **had been promoted to their Director's position**.

They followed the same process:
First, they chose the five main principles that would inspire their leadership, **if they were in the Director's position.**
Then, just like in the previous inquiries, they should give 5 points to the principle they would pay more importance to and 1 to that principle which was less important to them.

The purpose of the inquiries was to see **whether there was a similarity** between the principles the employees considered were applied by their **Director and those** they thought they would apply if appointed as Directors.

Following the inquiries **results**, the eleven groups were classified into **two** sub-groups depending on the **similarity of their answers.**
One sub-group, made up of **eigth groups** that we shall call "**Other Public Administrations**" and **another** formed of **three groups** that came

from one body called the "**Central Traffic Authority" (CTA)**

The first sub-group (eight groups) was formed of two groups of high-level employees and six groups of middle-level employees.

The second sub-group (three groups from CTA) was formed of high-level employees, as they were heads of the Provincial Traffic Units.

In each of the eight groups of the first sub-group, there was an average of 21 employees and in the 3 groups of ACT, an average of 18 employees.

The answers to the eight surveys by the first sub-group were very similar.

The same happened to the answers to the three surveys by the second sub-group.

But the answers from the **First** sub-group were **very different** from those given by the **Second** sub-group.

In the adjoin table it is possible to see the results of the enquiries of the two sub-groups: *"Other Public Administrations"* and *"Province Traffic Directors"*.

In each column, we can see the sum of the points given by the respondents to each criterion.

The first sub-columns (A and C) of each sub-group express the points obtained by the principles that the employees considered were the source of inspiration for the **behavior of the Director** in their respective Units (working center) .

The following columns **(B and D)** express the importance that the employees would give to those same principles on the hypothetical situation in which **they were appointed Directors of** their respective Units.

In the sub-group *"Other Public Administrations"*, the comparison, between the columns A and B, reflects the level of concordance or discrepancy between the criterions that **wer**e applied and the criterions that **should** have **been** applied, according to the enquired employees.

In the group *"Central Traffic Authority"* (CTA), the comparison, between the columns C and D reflects the level of concordance or discrepancy between the criterions that **wer** applied and the criterions that **should have been** applied, according to the enquired employees.

| PREFERRED GUIDELINES TO LEAD THE ORGANIZATION ||||||||
| GUIDELINES | Other Public Administrations ||| Province Traffic Directors |||
	A	B	A - B	C	D	C - D
Not cause conflicts	362	20	342	33	6	27
Effectiveness	244	209	35	92	85	7
Efficiency	147	243	-96	72	108	-36
Imparciality	39	47	-8	1	12	-11
Clarify rules	87	192	-105	32	40	-8
Respect rules	219	52	167	51	35	16
Clarify purposes	64	211	-147	19	41	-22
Stability	229	10	219	41	13	28
Expansion	78	39	39	16	17	-1
Client satisfaction	154	220	-66	93	94	-1
Encouraging creativity	24	130	-106	5	15	-10
Adjustment Technology	139	54	85	48	23	25
External image	357	30	327	80	52	28
Employees integration	35	151	-116	20	29	-9
Employees participation	27	152	-125	8	16	-8
Cooperation between employees	15	102	-87	2	5	-3
Salary satisfaction	15	90	-75	6	49	-43
Career advancement	27	92	-65	19	15	4
Human relations	21	65	-44	13	23	-10
Transparency	71	151	-80	50	38	12
Professionalization	118	168	-50	64	56	8
Conscience of social demands	57	110	-53	45	38	7

The table allows us to see that the employees of the group **"Other Public Administrations"** consider that **their Directors give priority to** the following leading principles in this order:
- Not cause Conflicts
- External Image
- Effectiveness (to reach the goal)
- Stability
- Respect the Rules

On the contrary, **if the employees were the Directors**, they would give priority to:
- Efficiency (Producing with less costs)
- Client Satisfaction
- Clarify the Organization's Objectives
- Effectiveness (to reach the goal)
- Clarify the Rules

We can notice the **great distance** between the directors' priorities, according to their employees' opinions, and those that the employees believed should be adopted.

They **only agree on one principle**: **Effectiveness**. But they fully disagree on the other principles to be applied.

If we analyze the quantitative **difference** between the points given, (see column A-B), **we can see the abyss between** what Directors do and what the employees believe they should do.

The employees believe that issues such "Not Cause Conflicts", "External Image" or "Organization Stability" should not be prioritized.

Of course, they do not reject "Not cause conflicts, External Image and Organization Stability" but they consider that they should **not be a priority** of the Public Administration.

Briefly, in the Sub-group "Others Public Administrations" the inquiry shows that the **employees believe that their directors mainly work on conservative and formal principles,** whereas they believe it is more important to give priority to the achievement of the results and the mission development.

Consequently, an important question arises to be pondered by the Manager/Leader of the organization: **if the employees disagree radically** with the main principles applied by their directors, to what extent can we expect them to contribute with their maximum potential to the organization?

The surveys carried out in the sub-group "Central Traffic Authority", **brought very different results.**

In this sub-group a **high concordance of criterions appeared** between the principles applied by the High Management of the Agency (TCA), as the Provincial Traffic directors who were enquired perceive them, and the principles that the Provincial Traffic directors would apply, if they were in positions of High Management in the Agency. (See the columns C and D of the table)

It can be underlined that the enquired Provincial Directors estimated that the High Management of the Agency gives priority to:
- Client Satisfaction
- Effectiveness
- External Image
- Efficiency
- Professionalism

On the other hand, the Provincial Directors estimated that if they occupied the High Management of the Agency, **they would also give priority to the same five main principles,** although with a slightly different order of priority.
- Effectiveness
- Client Satisfaction
- Efficacy
- Professionalism
- External Image

This great identity in the way of thinking, between the High Management of the Central Traffic Authority and its closest Internal Clients (the Provincial Traffic Directors), facilitates the communication and is **an ideal framework** in which the Provincial Directors can find a **trustful**

atmosphere to manifest their creativity and their management abilities.

Excellence wants the organizations to cultivate such an environment: **a context in which they pay attention and listen** to the Employees' (Internal Clients) opinions, using the appropriate tools to gather their points of view.

9.2.2 Providers as Internal Clients

The Providers are a special case of employees, a "sui generis" group. Any organization can expect, as it happened in the past, to be self-sufficient, creating departments dedicated to the production of all intermediary pieces or steps necessary in the production process.

Nevertheless, as reality has shown, **self-sufficiency is usually at the opposite pole of efficiency**.

Trying to produce all the intermediary products hinders the advantages of the specialization. It would be illogical if all organizations expected to have their own paper factory to produce the paper they need in the administrative process, or the cardboard for the packaging. It is much cheaper and less complex to buy paper and cardboard from specialized factories that work not only for one company, but also for the rest of the market.

Total Quality does not propose self-sufficiency, but teaches that all organizations **should consider their providers** as *"employees that have become independent"*, and provide from outside indispensable products or services.

Total Quality emphasizes the importance of establishing a trusting relationship with the companies that provide raw material, intermediary products or pieces necessary for the production processes of an organization.

Excellence in Management **rejects** the mercantilist approach that considers that the relation with the providers should be **founded exclusively on the price** of the products. Replacing a provider by another, only because the new provider offers a smaller price reduction, goes against the Excellence philosophy.

Before taking the decision to change the provider, it is necessary to reflect upon the following: *"in the case of a crisis, or unforeseen circumstances, who would be more willing to make an additional effort to serve the organization, the new provider or the company's old provider?"*

This does not mean that the company must maintain a passive attitude in a situation in which the prices of the usual providers are higher than those offered by other providers of similar products.

What Total Quality suggests in this case is to act with the provider in the same way they would act with an employee whose productivity is lower than that of his colleagues.

What would we do in this case? It would be logical to find the causes of the employee's low productivity, talk to him, analyze the case and find formulas meant to correct this situation. Only if there is no solution, due to causes attributed to the worker -such as being intentionally negligent or malicious- should the worker be used for another activity or be laid off.

It is convenient for the organization to maintain a **similar attitude with the providers.** Excellence claims that in the case of a decrease in competitiveness of prices, delivery regularity or post-sale assistance offered by the usual providers, the company should initiate conversations with them to find an alternative. Changing the provider, the ally, would be the last possible solution.

The main advantage of this approach is that **it generates loyalty** to the company by the providers. This can be very useful in many unforeseen circumstances (emergencies, sudden production increase, warehouse problems, etc.) that a company may confront.

Reality shows that nowadays most big companies have almost exclusive providers for each range of product. For example, Ford buys 95% of its parts from a few individual suppliers.

In 1997, Honorio Pertejo, General Director of Sogedac, a company that manages the purchases of the Peugeot Group in Spain, stated in the Madrid newspaper El Mundo: "*the habit of considering the provider like an enemy who comes to take all your money has been abandoned. Moreover, the sentiment of mutual collaboration has intensified... We cannot ask a provider to develop a new technology and then send him away in two or three days...In 1983 there were 741 providers; today there are 150".* Recently, in 2013, the Peugeot Group in Spain has repeated the same position.

These realities of Ford and Peugeot coincide with the philosophy that Total Quality proposes, as far as providers are concerned. TQM signals that **companies must see their providers as independent Internal Clients**, and their mutual relationship must go much further than a mere sale-purchase relation on the market.

9.3 Processes

Companies produce what clients buy. Studying the pool of external clients, we can get the X-ray of the entire productive organization.

Companies are what their clients are. The types and quantities of products sold to each client, the different types of delivery depending on each of them, the most frequent complaints, etc. all **define the activity** of the company and, in short, **what the company is doing to achieve its mission.**

The company creates and offers to its clients all its products and services through processes more or less defined.

The formalization of the manufacturing processes is extremely important when it comes **to normalized or standardized** products or services as it happens in many organizations.

In others cases, the formalization of processes is not so necessary.

Nevertheless, any kind of activity, including those that are apparently the simplest ones, is realized along a process and needs a series of entries or contributions (*inputs*) to produce the correct result (*output*): the requested product.

Let us consider the case of a person that **draws up a budget** by dictation. For this, he needs the following:

- Typewriter in good condition (typewriter or computer)

- Material (paper)
- Knowledge on how to handle the equipment
- Instructions on how to present the document
- Dictation of the content
- Revision with the help of the dictionary or a spell-check program to eliminate spelling mistakes
- Document biding or presentation
- Etc.

To obtain a correct product, all phases of the process must have been carried out correctly (dictation, writing, revision). Thus, for the example we are using, the person also needs:
- the existence of sufficient stock of paper
- the paper storing area must be protected against humidity so that the paper maintains its quality
- the computer or typewriter must be installed in an adequate position for its use by the person who is going to work at it
- the employee must have previous training for this kind of work, including in the budget not only the correct figures but also the presentation format that must be used
- etc.

Every employee is responsible for a larger or smaller number of phases of the process (even all the phases) that can be executed with more or less professional ability. **A previous good process**

design, including its control and supervision, **guarantees** that the final product will be a quality product and that it will accomplish the foreseen model or its specifications.

This happens both in the case of a normalized product and in the case of a non-standardized product (e.g. an environment study or the defense in a criminal lawsuit).

The need to define the process seems obvious when we want to carry out a complex activity, such as sending somebody to the Moon. Nevertheless, behind apparently simple productions (e.g. planting tomatoes) there are more or less complicated processes as well.

Frequently the quality problems of a certain product are found in the design of the production process itself. So, one of the factors that most guarantees the quality product is the in-depth analysis and revision of the corresponding production process.

Deming illustrated this statement with an anecdote. He said, *"Let us imagine a huge bowl in which we throw 50% of red balls and 50% of black balls. The employees handle mechanical 'ladles' that move all with the same speed and are introduced into the bowl to extract the little balls. Every employee makes the same number of extractions every hour. Out of the balls extracted by everyone, we count as good ones only those that are black. At the end of the working day, we calculate everybody's production and we see that some people extracted more black balls than others".*

Then the management **takes various decisions:** *awards those employees who took out more black balls, dismisses the ones that took out less black balls and offers a training course to everyone to improve their performance.*

During the **training course***, they are taught how the mechanical 'ladle' works and with what inclination it must be used. The employees practice with it and are encouraged to work with the greatest possible dedication.*

They get back to work and again it happens that an employee (not necessarily the same one as last time) takes out more black balls. The management **repeats its previous decisions***: award one, punish another and schedule more training courses for others.*

It is obvious that **with those decisions we cannot improve work quality**, as the origin of the problem lies in the initial introduction of the balls in the bowl.

If we eliminate all the red balls that enter the system, we will be eliminating all the red balls in the final product: **The problem started before the extraction process**. As it is obvious from the above example, the performance depends entirely on chance. The main problem of quality, in the aforementioned case, was the existence of (errors) faults in the design or in the process definition.

Deming points out that a situation similar to that expressed in the anecdote exists in many circumstances in real life: the employees are requested to obtain a quality product or service **that often does not depend on** good will, working capacity or on education or training.

As it was indicated, Deming estimates that, almost in all cases, 94% of the **problems are inherent to the system**, whereas only 6% can be attributed to the employee.

Juran estimates that 80% of production problems are due to the system and Ishakawa, in the same manner, points out that when the factory produces faulty items or flaws in a product, only 20 to 25% of the blame can be attributed to production line workers.

Therefore, how can we know whether the differences in the production per person, or in quality, are due to chance or not?

The conclusion is that **we must analyze the processes** to see if they are adequate to produce efficiently and with quality. From this analysis it is possible to see what phases need to be improved by redefining the process.

How should the processes be analyzed? **Who are** the ones that know all the intricacies of a process? Those who best know it are **the very workers** who execute it.

This leads us **back to the essential** proposal highlighted by Total Quality: **employees & workers must be involved** in the process, so that they feel it as their own and are eager to improve it constantly.

To reach this commitment, one of the main elements is to guarantee that they are going to keep their job positions.

It is essential for the workers to feel confident that the company will not fire them if the new improvements introduced reduce the need for positions in a production line, and that they will, at the most, be relocated in other lines of activity or in new lines that can be created.

Nowadays, it would seem possible to predict an era of labor instability, but the profound reality of the social-economic life is not heading towards that direction. We must not mistake the outsourcing of some company functions for the instability of the jobs of the employees in that same company.

Outsourcing consists in hiring another company to carry out functions that are not a company's basic mission. For example, the functions of cleaning, security, legal assistance, advertising, etc. in a construction company,

The rest of the company functions are the key company functions and must be carried out by the company itself since they represent the essence of its mission. To realize them, the company must have a permanent staff, except in those situations in which it must cope with top seasonal activities.

In a similar way, the employment in the companies that carry out outsourcing functions **must not necessarily be unstable**. In fact, for such companies, their activity is the nucleus of their mission. Therefore, they want to maintain a nucleus of trustful and specialized employees.

Obviously, the jobs are **more unstable** in the companies whose activity is done mainly by **non-specialized workers** who can be more easily hired as additional temporary staff.

The economic dynamism of modern society motivates the transformation of the company's mission in order to adapt it to the new market demands. Nevertheless, this does not imply necessarily employment instability. Reality shows that managers usually want to count on capable employees, loyal to them, and try to keep them **if they adapt to the new missions** assumed by the company.

Human beings' polyvalence offers many possibilities. Apart from those cases of radical changes in the activities that request an overspecialization, **it is possible to keep and reintroduce** loyal and dedicated employees in a new company.

The demands in terms of dynamism that Total Quality requests from the companies and the intense **cooperation** that it requests from the managers and employees are also a **guarantee of stability** in the work relations.

9.4 Continuous improvement

Continuous improvement is another fundamental pillar of the Excellence philosophy. **Corrective** measures **should not be** introduced **only after** the mistakes have taken place.

If **preventive** measures are introduced, then the errors will no longer be produced. The organization must make an effort to anticipate the errors or problems that may arise in the future.

Deming points out the fact that nobody questions the need for a constant improvement, but some believe that focusing on results (obtaining better results) will inexorably lead to improvements. For example, in his seminars Deming describes a female supervisor who, at the end of every working day, used to meet her staff to analyze what went wrong that day and to **discard all faulty products**.

The supervisor did everything possible to help every employee to avoid errors and improve their work. All her subordinates appreciated her and thought she had the best intentions.

It was true, but in time, the percentage of faulty products was constant. In the best case, Deming claims, she was wasting her time with her staff at the end of each working day.

What message does Deming want to convey?

What he wants to say is that in the aforementioned case, the supervisor was checking if the obtained products were in accordance with the specifications, which was not bad, **but was insufficient. The most important thing** is to revise whether the processes are adequate.

When problems are dealt with in a superficial way, we tend to lose confidence in the possibility of improvement, and this generates resentment and worsens things progressively.

Continuous improvement requires that:
- All employees should better **understand** the internal **processes** and the **clients'** needs
- The organization must have assumed the commitment to invest resources in order to **prevent** errors
- The human resources must have authority **to take or propose decisions that improve** quality in their own work domains.

Training for improvement should not be limited to high-level positions. Most likely, the executing staff knows better than their boss what goes on wrong in the front line and how to avoid it.

Therefore, it is necessary to guarantee a constant communication flow. It is not enough to exchange information once a year. Periodic reunions, where there is total freedom to formulate suggestions, are very important. If these requirements are not met, it is difficult to really have and maintain a shared and continuous improvement spirit.

The **improvement cycle** has **four stages**:
- The first one consists in deciding **what improvement** should be introduced in the functioning of the organization.
- The second one consists in applying the improvement at a **small scale** to see how it works.
- The third one consists in **commenting** the results of this improvement.
- The fourth one consists in deciding whether this improvement should be **extended** to other activities or, on the contrary, it would be best to abandon it because it has not produced the expected results.

Reality shows that many organizations **compare** their planning expectations to the results **just a few times.**

Very often, the assessment of the results of the plan, once approved, is not done. So the deviation from the plan and why it ocurred remain unknown.

Many times, plans are only part of a group of documents -really praised when formulated and presented- but hardly ever compared with the real results.

That is why, in section I, we emphasized the fact that Planning could be a good ally, but at the same time a fearful enemy.

The analysis of the differences between the plan and the goals obtained is an excellent and systematic source of information for improvement.

There are **three** ways to change an organization:
- The first one, with the help of **pressure** exerted **from outside** (for example, by a crisis in the sales)
- The second one consists in mere willfulness, with the best of intentions, but without a clear idea about *"why"* and *"where to go"*
- The third one consists in **becoming aware** of the fact that for any transformation, a new point of view is necessary. (**This way works best**).

The importance that the design of the processes has for the achievement of the adequate product or service **can lead to the error of thinking** that the essence of management consists in establishing **very detailed rules** that will allow the control of the functioning of the organization.

Ishikawa pointed out: *"there are people born to make rules. They are glad to establish norms to control the others and they believe that this is management"*

Ishikawa also points out *"if the norms and regulations are not revised every six months, it means that nobody is using them seriously"*

Excellence implies a **constant** questioning of all processes and all products or services, by asking continuously: **Can they be improved?**

It is not enough to tell the employees: *"Let's formulate suggestions"* and that is it. It is not enough to say it only once.

It is necessary **to encourage them continuously** to offer contributions and suggestions, **by thanking** them for their proposals, no matter how useful they are, **and guaranteeing the employees that** their suggestions/proposals will be analyzed, assessed and implemented, if the case may be.

In order to promote a continuous improvement, **it is essential to thank the**

employee for presenting an improvement suggestion, informing them whether it will be implemented or not, and explaining the reasons why.

The four major lines for improvement are:
- Innovation of products and services
- Innovation in processes that generate products or services
- Improvement of products or services
- Improvement of current processes

Sometimes it is hard to make a clear distinction between innovation and improvement. Innovation implies a qualitative leap, whereas improvement has a more limited and gradual nature within the process or product.

Continuous improvement needs the creation of a dynamic process that promotes what today is called *"management of knowledge",* that is, to obtain benefit from managing all the knowledge and ideas possessed by the employees.

In other words, it means managing the enterprise knowledge, which often resides in the sum of the knowledge possessed by individuals.

In everyday work, or in the relation with the clients, the employees discover things that are not working and, in many cases, they find alternatives for improvement. However, nobody asks them about it. **Quite often people are just waiting for an opportunity to express their opinions.**

There is a potential knowledge that a good manager should know how to manage. General George Patton used to say, *"Never tell people how to do things. Tell them what you want to achieve and they will surprise you with their talent"*

10 BENCHMARKING

Continuous improvement must not be based only on the internal effort of the organization. It is absurd to expect that all innovations should be the fruit of the internal creativity in the organization. **We must learn from the external environment**; we must be willing to assimilate all the positive contributions, no matter where they come from.

One thing is to show a strong will for improvement that makes the organization change for the better and another is to think that any idea for improvement must come from inside the organization.

We are living in a very dynamic and complex world and this means that inter-dependence is higher every day.

The big automotive companies only produce a maximum of 30% of the parts that make up a car. The improvement of most of the car parts (70%) and its manufacturing processes take place in the supplying companies.

Providers generate many of the improvements: new technologies, new materials, new products and services. This forces all factories to adapt their manufacturing processes to all these new materials, technologies or intermediate products.

Excellence points out the fact that the manager of any organization must play the role of a person that is **continuously looking ahead**, trying to find new ideas, new suggestions.

Much of the success that the organizations achieve in conquering new markets derive from having taken the initiative to introduce, in the production processes, new technologies **that come from outside,** or to have made new products based on the new materials created by the providers.

> Benchmarking = Comparing one organization to others

Other companies or organizations, very similar to ours, also come up with many ideas for improvement. That is why **it is very important to know what they are doing, why, how, etc.**

Therefore, it is necessary to ask questions such as:
- How can we find out whether our organization is using its improvement potential?
- Are we better than our counterparts or rivals?
- What aspects are we better in?

- How can we improve our performance?
- And most important, in what aspects are they better than us?

Our great challenge is to learn from those who are the best.

Benchmarking is, in essence, a systematic method to **obtain information and learn from others**, from the outside, from the environment.

The word *benchmark* means **a point or a reference level** with which to compare ourselves. Companies use Benchmarking, the establishment of reference points to compare themselves in key areas to the best companies in the world.

Today, every company can meet other similar companies with which to compare themselves. Even the companies acting in a monopoly regime can always meet similar companies in other countries or in other economic sectors in the world.

Without benchmarking, the organization may become narrow-minded and self-satisfied. It may think that it is following a good improvement pace. But, is it true?

Benchmarking brings a vision on possible results, it offers an understanding of **how to reach** them and an **objective** to target and surpass.

10.1 What characteristics can be compared?

All parameters defining an organization, such as its organizational structure, type of management, material and human resources and results, can be measured and compared.

Thus, we can compare:
- Clients' degree of satisfaction
- Sales volume
- Investment in Research and Development (Eg.Training)
- Acquisition system (Number of providers, punctuality in the delivery of the products, etc)
- Management of stocks
- Length of time for the design of new products
- Products or services per person, productivity
- Etc.

The benchmarking program **must focus on the key activities** of a company.

We must avoid collecting an excessive volume of information.

On one hand, due to the **cost** that it implies, and on the other hand, because it is **better to focus on the key aspects** of other companies that make it possible for them to exhibit higher production indicators or more efficient organization forms.

How can we identify those activities where it is convenient to do *benchmarking first*?

There are different methods to see what these sectors are:

- **Polls among clients** inquiring in what areas of activity they see comparative advantages that might lead them to turn to our competitors
- **Function analysis.** It shows us what activities of our organization consume most resources, and consequently, where it would be most convenient to promote improvements.
  As it is obvious, the growth by 5% of productivity in an area that concentrates 80% of the human and material resources in an organization will be much more profitable, in quantitative terms, than the growth by 15% of the productivity in the rest of the company that consumes just 20% of human and material resources
- **Cost analysis for each activity** (a version of functional analysis) identifies the activities that have most costs and especially the ones in which the added value (the cost of the process) is higher. Therefore, it will be more profitable to introduce improvements in

efficiency or revise processes in those areas than to do so in the rest of the organization.

After choosing the key areas of activity of which we want to get information from other companies, it is necessary to precise the **key comparison parameters** we are looking for, such as:
- number of projects drawn up
- average cost per drawn-up project
- number of projects carried out and their cost
- average cost per carried-out project
- number of granted licenses
- number of paid invoices
- number of transported passengers/kms
- etc.

Logically, every organization must define, depending on its specific **activities,** the most significant **parameters** of its functioning processes, organization and **results** to compare them to those of similar organizations.

Once we have defined what information we want to gather, we should decide:
- **Where we can get the data** about what is happening in other organizations
- **Which we can use** as a model to establish the reference standards
- **How we can obtain** this information

There are **several possibilities**:
1. From **similar Units** in the same **organization**. For example, when a car maker has two or more factories that manufacture the same type of vehicles, either in the same country or in different countries.

2. From **similar Units** in other organizations operating in **non-competitive areas** or markets. For example, from different municipalities in the same country that exchange data on key reference parameters, such as the number of citizens related to the number of policemen, number of formalities per civil servant, the staff in the administrative department compared to the rest of the departments, the number of construction licenses and the average price of construction works, etc.

3. From **non-similar Units** in our **own organization**. This sometimes does not allow reaching conclusions very easily. For example, the degree of computerization in the human resources department compared to that in the economic management department, or in the general service department, etc.

4. **From the competitors**. It is usually more difficult to get data, although nowadays there are many general indicators that go public. For example, the volume of units sold, staff, passengers per km, etc, which allow, at least, the comparison of the big indicators.

5. From companies **whose activities are in different areas from ours**. It is easier to exchange information and visits and there are always common elements, at least in the administrative areas, from which interesting conclusions can be drawn.

10.2 How to collect the adequate information

Getting *benchmarking* data implies an effort that can be made by our own organization or through external assistance.

The first step is to identify the adequate companies or organizations we want to compare with ours. They should be organizations that show a high level of productivity or quality. They may be identified by asking the clients, consultants, theoreticians, civil servants, associations or entities specialized in getting indicators, etc.

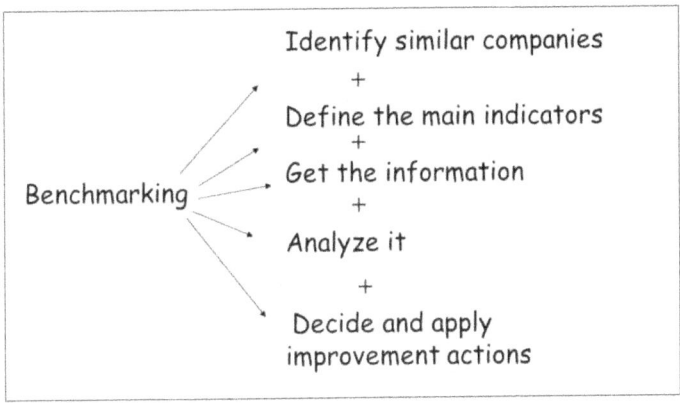

Secondly, it is necessary to obtain **concrete data.** That will be more or less difficult depending on the possibilities to access data about the functioning and results of other companies.

In any case, the **sources of information** are multiple and varied.

Some of them are **indirect**, such as technical magazines, trade associations, chambers of commerce, client questionnaires, etc.

Others are **direct**: through the exchange of information at national or international level with organizations that do not enter in direct competition with us. In this sense, fairs, trade shows and congresses of the organizations in the same sector are very good scenarios where to find information.

Total Quality Management does not oppose the collection of benchmarking data by external consultants.

However, as TQM underlines, the commitment of the organization to the improvement process and the members of the organization, including the ones that take major decisions and specialists in the main processes, all must contribute to define the **indicators** that they consider more valuable for benchmarking comparison.

This very group of company employees must also cooperate to **identify the organizations** that achieve high levels of productivity and collect data about the activities and ratios of these organizations.

If the company opts for hiring an external consultant to do this search, the provided data and conclusions must be checked to guarantee that they correspond to what was requested.

The group must calculate the indicators of the activity within the own organization, compare them with the *benchmarking* data, identify what must be learnt and design a plan to implement them.

10.3 Benchmarking data collection. Recommendations

1. It is an **expensive activity**, especially when it is done in very opaque organizations or in organizations that are not willing to share information. It is necessary to think and plan how to do it very well.

2. We must **avoid collecting too much** information as there is a risk of not using most of it.

3. It is necessary not only to compare production data, **but also to study the processes,** which frequently require communication, direct or indirect, with the staff of the other organization.

4. It is **only worth paying attention** to activities that improve the client's satisfaction level or those that have direct consequences over the profits. Other data, such as parking spaces per civil servant, numbers of holidays, etc. are secondary and one must not dedicate time looking for this information, at least in the first phase of the *benchmarking*.

10.4 In what moment is it good to use reference levels?

It must be done in **all the phases** of the company life, including the moment in which the activity is created or sets off.

In fact, the indicators of other organizations are useful especially **when the organization is created** or **when a profound reform** of re-launching of the organization is done, because at this particular moment, key decisions that influence, in the long term, the development of the organization are taken.

At any other moment, the benchmarking process is also useful because the knowledge of the indicators coming from excellent companies offers us clues regarding strategies that can help our organization to evolve. The benchmarking indicators are always a stimulus for the improvement of the company.

In France, one of the main methods used successfully by the Agricultural Service to advise agricultural companies and farmers was benchmarking data obtained from different agricultural companies or farmers. Data such as kilograms of fertilizers per hectare, quantity and type of seeds used, types and horsepower of the tractors, number of animals per hectare, etc.

This method has been used for a long time. The French Agricultural Service compensated the companies and farmers that provide the benchmarking information with a more direct technical support, more consultancies and a special treatment, apart from guaranteeing them total confidentiality regarding the information, even in front of the Internal Revenue Service.

10.5 Benchmarking limits

1. It does not indicate by itself what clients want. The *benchmarking* process offers information about the current reality, but nothing about the clients' desires or expectations. If a product is old-fashioned, no improvement in the production process will turn it into a competitive one. It can be cheaper, but it will always be old-fashioned.

The *benchmarking* process never replaces the polls about the new products the clients may want, nor can it substitute the processes of innovation and creation of new products made by our own company.

2. It leads us to focus on the improvement of the aspects of the **already existing processes.** We may make the mistake of focusing too much on copying what others have and less on innovation, disregarding the creative potential in our company.

That is why it is necessary to look outside **and at the same time** act creatively inside.

3. It is only a first step. The company can only improve if the changes are implemented. It is not enough to obtain the indicators. It is necessary to meditate on them and to be committed to push our company to reach or surpass, within the shortest time possible, the ratios of the top organizations in our activity sector.

4. The practice of the *benchmarking* process mainly **identifies the differences** between production levels, **but not how** they are reached by others companies.

It is imperative to obtain complementary information about the processes carried out in the organizations that have the best results. This information may be more difficult to obtain.

Nevertheless, the adequate research has to be done in order to learn **how our competitors work** and what the differences regarding production processes, organizational structure, culture and others are from our organization.

11 QUALITY COSTS

Every organization is exposed to experiencing multiple errors and failures in all the processes (strategic, operational or support processes) designed to achieve its mission.

This happens in the industry and in the service sectors. This happens as well in both the public and private sectors.

The errors and failures have consequences that cause setbacks with respect to both the economic results, the image of the organization, and to society as a whole.

Companies and organizations should care about providing the customers with **faultless and flawless products and services,** with products that really meet the expected characteristics, in order to avoid the situation in which a client feels cheated for having received a product or a service that shows an inferior quality to the one announced.

To ensure this standard, it is necessary to invest human and material resources. This investment **implies certain costs** that are named "**costs of quality assurance**" or, more simply, "**quality costs**".

Lesley Munro Faure, in his book *"Implementing Total Quality Management"* defines quality costs as *"those incurred by a company to ensure that the total service offered to a customer conforms to the specifications required by the customer"*

The "**production costs**" of products or services implies a diversified group of costs that we could classify as follows:
- Product study and design costs
- Processes and organization design costs
- Production costs, including control
- Delivery costs
- Costs for repairing or remedying the complaints received
- Etc.

By "**quality-assurance**" costs, we mean
- **Prevention** costs to avoid errors in the production process
- **Control** costs meant to guarantee the product adequacy
- **Repair** costs to remedy the faults that may arise.

11.1 Functioning costs and quality costs

The functioning costs of an organization can be broken down in three component groups:

C_1= costs associated **directly** to the product or service **production**. It includes all the costs directly involved in the production process. It also includes the costs of default products and the subsequent costs related to remedy the faults (receive, remedy and re-send the remedied product)

C_2= costs associated with **support** activities (organization, planning, design, etc.) that are not directly productive, but that can reduce production costs and improve the product design.

These support costs relate to, for example, the time spent reflecting or discussing how to eliminate duplication, avoid bureaucratization, reorder the processes, reorganize the units, improve the physical layout of machines, etc.

C_3= **hidden** costs due to underuse of resources and missed opportunities.

Example, a secretary who spends 30 minutes looking for his boss is a wasted cost. An employee wishing to collaborate and not being involved in the work process is another example of wasted cost.

Other examples of **hidden cost**:
- The costs involved in an employee's high turnover, due to lack of motivation
- The costs of training a new employee, such as the costs involved in using experienced employees to help, assist and train new ones

- The impact on production and quality loss, due to skilled workers and supervisors who leave their jobs
- The costs involved in the recruitment of new personnel
- Etc.

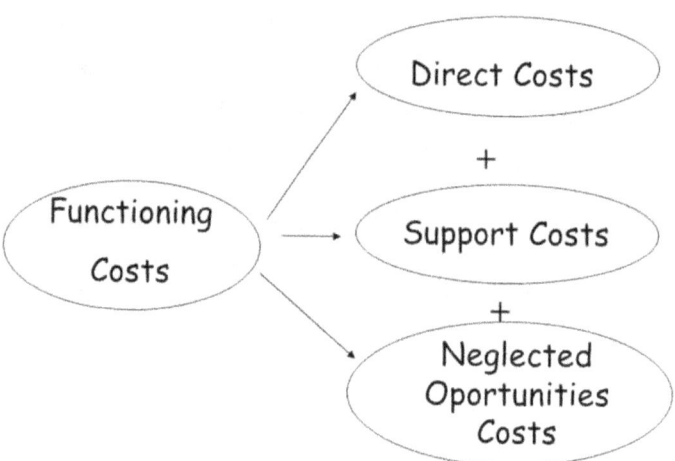

If efforts are made to avoid under-use of resources, both material and human, it is possible to achieve significant savings, in all types of organizations.

Another way to classify the components of the **functioning costs** in an organization would be the following:

- **quality** cost (prevention and control)

- **non-quality** cost (external and internal failures)
- cost of the **execution** of what has been done without faults.

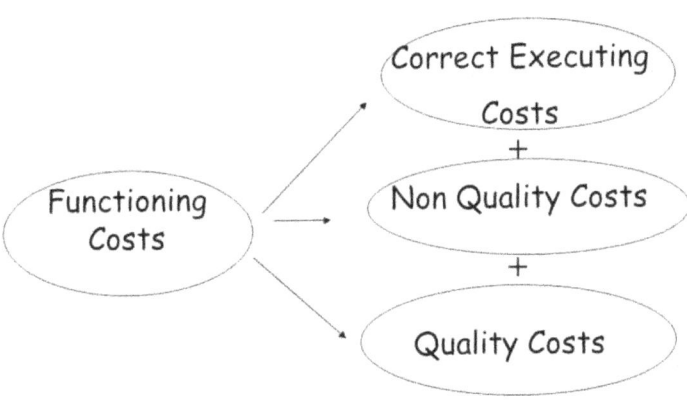

In this line, Rosander considers that, indeed, the total Quality Costs are the sum of **Quality costs** and **Non-Quality** costs.

Total Quality Costs, would consist of two parts:
- Costs assumed to guarantee quality, like the **Prevention** and **Control** costs
- Costs of activities, which do not produce quality, such as the costs due to internal and external **Failures**

Rosander defines each of these types of costs as follows:

Costs of Prevention. These are the costs of actions taken to prevent producing poor quality products or services.

They include the costs of activities such as the selection and hiring of enough qualified staff at all levels; the design and delivery orientation and training workshops; special training programs; costs of personnel dedicated to improve quality; planning; data collection and analysis; quality reports on the organization; etc.

Control costs. They are the costs incurred in the **detection** of errors and to ensure that the final product or service has a good quality.

Inspection costs, review, verification, testing, auditing, sampling, cost analysis of products and services, etc. are included in this group of control costs.

Costs caused by Internal Failures. They are all the costs involved in the **correction** of mistakes and failures made in the processes realized **within** the organization.

They include the costs to correct methods, procedures or faulty techniques and the cost to correct errors and failures in the products or services.

For example, the cost of material consumed in the errors and failures; the cost of having underused equipment; time lost by employees; time spent correcting errors; poorly written manual and instructions that need correction; deficient or erroneous explanations; time spent to re-do a job that has been poorly done; the cost of inadequate training; the cost of absenteeism, etc.

Cost caused by External Failures. They are the costs involved in the **correction of** mistakes or failures that arise once the product or service is **outside** the organization.

For example, when customers discover and report flaws. Costs such as those dedicated to receiving complaints from customers; receiving, storing and repairing defective products returned by the customer; fixing bugs and errors in the service provided; costs of forwarding the repaired product to the customer; compensations; negative impact on customers; lost customers; bad image to other clients, etc...

One of the objectives of any organization that wants to improve or head towards excellence is to eliminate the so-called non-quality costs. The structure, in percentage, of the total costs associated with quality, highlights the difference between a total quality organization and one that is not.

In the next table, we can see that **the organizations that work under the Excellence concentrate** most part of the so-called quality costs **on the prevention and control costs**. Costs due to internal and external faults represent a smaller percentage.

An organization that works under the Excellence has a different percentage structure of quality costs. In addition, its quality costs by unit of product should be inferior to those in other organizations that are not quality-oriented.

This quality costs reduction is an important **savings** that justifies the phrase: **"Quality is cheap"**

Costs Framework		
COSTS	UNADEQUATE	ADEQUATE
Prevention	10%	40-50%
Control	20%	40-50%
Internal Failures	40%	0-10%
External Failures	30%	0-10%

Any policy for improvement in any organization faces the problem of having to quantify **the results of the improvements**.

Talking about Excellence may sound nice but the President of a company may want to know what, in economic terms, has been achieved, after creating a Department of Excellence or TQM.

He may want to know to what extent the results of the improvements outweigh the costs involved after the creation of this Department.

Every manager has the right and duty to ask these questions and to demand specific answers to them.

Detailed information about the quality costs of the company **helps to explain** quantitatively the results of the improvement process.

The evolution of the quality **percentage structure**, in comparison to the starting point, should show the emphasis on quality and its impact on reducing the cost of non-quality.

The decrease in total costs of quality (quality + no quality) is, in a special way, a clear expression of the impact that the introduction of quality has had (apart from other benefits such as the improvement in the image of the company, the sales increase, etc.)

The companies that do not focus on quality **do not usually calculate separately** the costs of quality but include them within the so-called production costs or, what is worse, in the so-called company's general costs. So, important information is missed.

The **general** costs are often a *"tailor's box"* in which both, the **support** costs, such as accounting or staff management, security, cleaning, etc. and the costs of **dealing with** complaints, storage, repair defective products, customer service, etc are thrown. In this case, the company does **not become aware** of the amount of its **non-quality costs.**

A problem that often occurs in many organizations is that even the production cost of the goods or services are **unknown** to most managers.

The Spanish manager Lopez de Arriortúa tells that during his time as Head of Production at General Motors in Zaragoza (Spain), he had a car (Opel Corsa) disassembled in all its pieces which later were placed in a room on a large table, each piece with a label expressing its cost.

Then, along with his management team, he devoted a lot of time to study each of those pieces to understand their individual cost. It was the starting point of an intense reflection on what to do in order to lower their cost, and in this way decrease the total production cost.

Unfortunately, within the companies (and in the Public Administration) the knowledge that the managers have of the production costs for every good or service is often rather reduced.

A Gallup poll carried out in 1986 among 698 directors of various companies regarding quality costs proved that 23% of the directors did not know the production costs of services and products, not to mention the internal structure of those costs (execution costs + quality costs+ non-quality costs).

This fact led them to have groundless opinion about quality costs.

Thus, 70% of the managers estimated the expenses caused by low quality (errors, failures, registering complaints, remedy faults, etc.) as being 10% or less of gross sales.

Still, the real non-quality costs, as it is reflected by studies and specialists' experiences, in many cases represents a much higher figure, between 25% and 40% of the sales percentage.

No doubt, one of the reasons why the non-quality costs are ignored is because 64% of those managers measured quality only from the point of view of the number of complaints, **but without real knowledge of the costs** involved to deal with those complaints.

Moreover, they did not take into consideration other important information, such as the number of unhappy clients that did not file a complaint but who stopped buying the company's products and started to make bad publicity to the company.

Neither had they assessed the cost of the resources and of the insufficiently used company potential and talent.

TQM option implies not only the theoretical knowledge about what can be improved but also the awareness of the amount of the possible reduction of costs and, consequently, of the increase of possible benefits, that may derive from the reductions of costs.

The ideal goal is to reduce the costs of internal and external faults to zero, increasing the resources allocated to control, and especially to prevention.

The aim is to prevent the occurrence of non-quality costs. The more you spend in control and prevention the lower the amount of costs due to failures. Ideally, the failure costs should go down to zero. This is a goal that every ambitious quality program should have on the horizon.

11.2 Non-Quality Costs

The costs of non-quality are the costs produced by applying **wrong or unnecessary actions or generating bad products.**

The non-quality costs are also known as **unadjusted costs** (or costs of **non-compliance** with what was necessary and useful to do) They are all those costs of making an inadequate or useless work (e.g. a report that nobody reads; excess stocks; surplus production capacity; loss of opportunities; unmotivated employees, etc)

Other non-quality costs are those for not having done the job properly from the very first moment. (e.g. costs of repairs or replacement parts, product return costs; costs of handling complaints; compensation, etc.).

In addition, non-quality costs are those corresponding to unnecessary activities: the costs of activities that are not profitable for the organization, such as meetings without a clear purpose, repetitive information, useless data, etc.

The non-quality costs can be used as an indicator for selecting the areas in which improvement must be a priority.

Those activities, or processes, **in which high costs of NON-quality are detected**, are the areas where a most urgent action for improvement needs to be taken.

11.3 How Will Non-Quality Costs Be Calculated?

All costs associated with an activity should be considered as a part of the total operating costs.

The sum of the costs of the activities that are carried out in an organization represents the **cost of the functioning** of that organization.

The key costs are:

- Direct work
- Indirect work
- Direct materials
- Occupancy, space, light,
- Administrative Support (Payroll, storage)
- Amortization of equipment

The costs of each activity can be broken down into the above types of costs. **In each** of those types of costs, **non-quality costs can exist as well.**

The Functional Analysis allows us to see the structure of the organization in types of activities.

For a functional analysis it is convenient to:
- Disaggregate the organization in **production Units**, considering as such both the units that generate the final products or services and those that are in charge of supporting activities.
- Disaggregate the operation of each of those production units in **productive activities**, answering the following question: What products does each Unit generate? This is equivalent to having an X-ray of the unit through its activities.

Once we have classified the various activities involved in each u**nit, we must identify** the **possible causes for non-quality** in each of these activities.

This information is collected primarily **from the employees** performing the activities and **from the customers** who buy the products or services. Both are the main source of useful information.

We can study all activities to work out the non-quality costs in each of them. This study requires a certain level of experience, imagination and creativity.

Sometimes we may come across activities whose non-quality costs **seem impossible to calculate**. For example, how to calculate the costs of non-quality of a Unit dedicated to creative designs or original ideas.

One might consider, as non-quality costs, the costs of the **designs that are not implemented, as well as** those costs arising from the **changes introduced once** the design has entered the production phase.

To what extent, should the time spent until someone comes up with a brilliant new idea, be computed as a non-quality cost?

Sometimes, the new idea appears after a long period of thinking and reflecting. At other times, it comes up all of a sudden. Therefore, it is not easy to calculate the costs of non-quality of an area of Innovation & Development.

If the period of thinking and reflection has been used efficiently, it would not be fair to say that the length of time until a new idea appears is a non-quality cost. But it is a cost.

In the production Units, we should keep it in mind that, in many cases, some intended control costs **are indeed non-quality costs** because they do not add value.

As an example, in the Public Administration the proposals or decisions often include a pyramid of signatures that very frequently are merely **formal signatures, formal control,** representing hierarchical positions, which do not provide any real supervision.

We should also consider as non-quality costs, those **costs of control that are higher** than the amount of the expenditure controlled. Sometimes the wages of the staff that controls the expenditure on taxis are higher than the total amount of expenditures on taxis. In this case, it seems clear that the system of control and its costs are non-quality costs.

The calculation of non-quality costs may encounter opposition from employees, if they feel that these calculations are a threat to keeping their jobs. **Only if the employees are confident that**

they will not be laid off, will they be willing to disclose or recognize which of the functions they perform are useless.

Nobody, in a healthy mind, throws stones at their own job. If an employee is afraid of being dismissed, he will not recognize that his tasks are useless or that he has little workload. Consequently, **only in a climate of trust,** will the **employees be willing to collaborate in the detection and removal of non-quality costs** generated in their working environment.

The organization should promote the employee collaboration. To do this, it must feel responsible to relocate the redundant staff from one activity to another.

The employee may accept the trauma of having to change his job in the interest of greater efficiency in the organization but he will never accept that his job be threatened by a possible dismissal. In such a context, he will not cooperate to detect flaws in the production process.

Excellence is incompatible with the job-reduction programs, except in the case of an acute crisis, and even then, the crisis should be explained to the whole staff and they should be involved in the process of finding possible solutions.

Therefore, **TQM organizations are usually better prepared** to cope with a possible economic crisis because they have adopted a permanent creative and fore sighting mindset.

One of the main responsibilities of the Quality Improvement Department is to **design a quality and non-quality costs identification methodology** for the organization.

This methodology should be **based on a global vision** of the components cost of the organization (staff, location, material consumption, equipment, etc.) to avoid the frequent **mistake of becoming obsessed with reducing small sources** of costs such as: excessive use of the photocopier, electricity, phones, etc.

This does not mean ignoring the small items of cost but **focusing primarily on the big ones** and leaving for later the task of checking on those that have less impact overall.

This conception of focusing on what is most important implies **two aspects**:
1. **Do not pursue absolute precision** when calculating non-quality costs. In many cases, we will have to make cost estimation. There will also be non-quality components that will be found out later. To impel the improvement process, an **approximate**

calculation is much more valuable today than a very exact one, obtained in a year's time.

2. **The introduction of the improvements is to be carried out gradually**. We should **obtain** information and suggestions **today**. Later on, they will be refined, new non-quality costs will be detected and the corresponding improvements will be introduced.

The figures of non-quality costs are especially meant to inform the organization and all employees about the potential for improvement. They should never be used to threaten the people suspected of being responsible for non-quality-costs with punishments or sanctions.

Let us remember once again that Excellence believes that the main cause of errors resides in the system itself not in the individual.

The non-quality cost figures must be used **to stimulate the top management** to believe in the potential of TQM and to support its implementation.

The figures of non-quality costs must be used to encourage the employees to find better solutions in a climate of trust, loyalty and cooperation.

Rosander indicates the following **examples of non-quality costs**:

A. Non-quality costs within the company or organization.

Production errors: time and costs implied
- The time elapsed until the error is discovered
- The time elapsed until the error is corrected
- The time used to remedy the cause-effect chain that produced the error
- The costs of letters, phone calls and shipments made to remedy the errors
- The costs derived from disasters and accidents.

Faults in the deliveries received:
- Cost to discover the flaws
- Effect chain: clients' complaints
- Costs of the accidents and disasters caused by the fault items received.

Time wasting or badly employed:
- Time wasting (staff cost)
- Time wasting (equipment cost)
- Time wasting (maintenance cost)

Clients' complaints:
- Complaint-system costs (request reception, answer and solution)
- Law suits for damage and product responsibility.

Lost clients:
- Annual loss due to lost of clients
- Losses generated by the effect of lost clients in other possible clients.

Employees' attitudes and behaviors:
- Company image prejudice
- Lost clients
- Lost sales
- Lost working time
- Administrative costs which are unnecessary

Unnecessary investments:
- Unused equipment
- Unused external consultancy
- Inadequate software

B. Non-quality costs on the client
Fixing errors:
- Displacement costs, phone calls or letter costs
- Cost of the time used by the client to explain the problem to the company

Getting repairs done:
- Clients' waiting time
- Clients' time wasted instead of being at their work or business.

12 QUALITY CIRCLES or IMPROVEMENT GROUPS

Many organizations manifest obvious problems that seem easy to solve. Then, **why is it so difficult** to correct them? That happens **because nobody takes responsibility** for doing it. Nobody is specifically in charge of improvements.

All managers agree with the following motto: *"Let's improve constantly our production system, our products and services"*

Nevertheless, **do the organizations act under this premise?**

Have they established procedures to collect information and opinions about their products and services?

Have they established effective channels to collect the suggestions from their employees and clients?

Do these channels work?

Are the suggestions analyzed and answered by anyone?

Is this information passed on to the technicians and process designers?

Do they use it?

Is there a concrete person in charge of passing the suggestions to the technicians and designers?

Etc.

Fred Taylor proposed, in the early twentieth century, a way to implement improvements: to create a Unit of Rationalization, Organization and Methods, in charge of studying thoroughly the processes and procedures, and propose and implement improvements.

The workers should apply the new processes, while the Rationalization Unit would be in charge of looking for improvements and implementing them.

Is this still the appropriate way to proceed? Are the experts in organization and processes the only suitable persons to suggest improvements?

Have the employees any knowledge or ideas to contribute to the improvement or are they just agents who apply them?

To what extent is the Taylorist Philosophy valid nowadays to manage the employees' knowledge and talent?

TQM advocates a radically different solution from the one offered by Taylor.

TQM focus on the employee's collaboration through the so-called Quality Circles **(from now on QCs).** The wrong way to manage the past Quality Circles led them to rejection. Then, their name changed to Improvement Groups. Nevertheless, its essence and importance and working methods are still valid today.

12.1 What are Quality Circles?

They are groups of employees, from the same or different areas of activity, who meet regularly to identify problems, propose solutions, implement improvements and new processes, and assess the progress of the measures that were already taken.

The QC emerged from the experience of Japanese management. It should be noted that it was in this country where the TQM philosophy first took root, due to the intense group feeling that characterizes Japanese culture.

In Japanese organizations, the employees first consider themselves members of a team, and then they see themselves as individuals. So they focus on the interest of the whole rather than on their own personal interest. In this context, the ideas of Deming found an excellent breeding ground.

In the Japanese culture, employees consider new ideas, innovations and improvements as a **by-product of working together**. Most processes of improvement are the result of sharing experiences and observations during the performance of their duties.

Institutionalized regular meetings of employees to suggest improvements were not but a natural way to channel their commitment to the company. Traditional Japanese attitude of giving priority to the interests of the community has weakened in the latest generations, influenced by the individualism of the West, but this spirit remains in many organizations and in Japanese culture in general.

This participatory structure of employees to suggest improvements was transferred to the West under the name of Quality Circles (QC)

However, the experience has shown that it is **not enough to create a structure** to make the TQM work in the same way that it is not enough to put a suggestion box for suggestions to proliferate.

In the 70's and 80's, the QC was introduced in the UK but many of them failed. It seems that the main cause of this failure was that the QC was left alone, as if the mere creation of the QCs would naturally improve quality.

Nevertheless, they did not have enough authority, nor training to solve significant problems, so, in many cases, the QC members lost interest and the QC disappeared.

In the United States, almost all attempts to create Quality Circles have been a fiasco.

American managers have been more interested in acknowledging who has the merit for good results or, on the other hand, in blaming for failures —with the help of the information collected and the analysis made by the QCs- rather **than**

introducing a real tool for the improvement of the system.

They expected that quality would improve just by the mere creation of the QCs. That was an error: Excellence does not work **if the essence of its philosophy is not understood and applied.**

One feature of this philosophy is that the fundamental effort in the implementation of TQM corresponds to the company's management.

Even when Excellence has been introduced, the effort and momentum from the management remains critical. **If the management does not support the QCs** in a clear and unambiguous way, if it does not give them power and autonomy, the QCs will fail.

Excellence considers that the management of **human resources is the most difficult issue** of a management as it involves promoting the development of employees' talent, using their competences and creativity, giving them opportunities, promoting, motivating and giving them co-responsibility.

There is a function that cannot be delegated and that applies only to the leader. **The manager should at least follow closely the Excellence implementation** and support it to ensure that all areas and all the staff work together as a team. An orchestra can serve as an example. The director is responsible for ensuring that all performers work in a coordinated manner.

The role of the manager or leader is to ensure that everyone in the QC works together, and that the QC works harmoniously with the rest of the organization to achieve its objectives. The manager must inspire the QC with a spirit of constructive cooperation and should leave it unmistakably clear that cooperation is the indispensable standard under which they must operate.

Constituted under these assumptions, each QC is a group of employees **who, together, feel committed and also encouraged** to analyze all the problems and suggest solutions. It is very important that individuals, with experience from the various areas involved, participate in the design and implementation of the improvements.

The membership of each Quality Circle should not be excessive (no more than 6-8 persons) so that they can have a flexible and participatory dialogue. Every teamwork involves an effort that must be simplified to the maximum, adopting a **working methodology** that makes it as light as possible. Group size is a key factor, although not the only one, to ensure smooth operation.

Each QC should have a member elected by the QC itself **to run it**. This person must energize the team and inspire it to achieve concrete results.

His role is often difficult to perform and requires experience and special conditions. The position of a team leader can rotate among members of the QC as this also serves as an experience for every member to get a better understanding of the features, benefits and challenges of teamwork.

12.2 Philosophy of Quality Circles

In the management of every human group, a matter of substance arises: Is it possible **to find a point of equilibrium** in which the whole respects the individual, and, at the same time, the individual considers the interests of the whole as part of his own self-interest?

Erich Fromm, in his famous book *"The Fear of Freedom"*, showed that the exaltation of the individual's freedom, in the sense often used as *"doing whatever one pleases"* ends up causing individual insecurity and dissatisfaction.

Indeed, this extreme approach of freedom leads individuals to fear the *"freedom"* that other people enjoy, because it could eventually be brought against them. Therefore, freedom ends up being perceived as a threat rather than a framework for self-realization.

Many philosophers and thinkers have addressed this issue and, in general, have concluded that it is necessary to repress freedom, to a certain extent, to ensure social order.

Hobbes's phrase "*man is a wolf to man*" is still shared by many. If it is essentially true, social life would be a more or less civilized jungle, where it would be always necessary to be on the defensive against possible attacks by other human predators.

Such a concept induces the individual to be afraid of freedom, willing to sacrifice part of it, in order to be accepted by a *"flock"* and feel protected as a member of a community.

Obviously, says Fromm, this situation is not ideal since it requires the individual to give up part of his freedom so as to be integrated in a *"ghetto"*. That forces the individual to accept the rules of the "*ghetto*", even when he does not agree with its ideals and principles.

The next step is that the individual does not question the rules that are imposed in order to feel welcome in the group. In this case he is renouncing to the full freedom of being himself in exchange for the protection received by becoming a member of the *"flock"*.

In this *"ghetto"*, that may even be a social majority, its members strive to maintain the hallmarks that differentiate them from other groups and collectivities and they defend the *"ghetto"* professional or business interests or beliefs.

There is nothing wrong with joining a group close to oneself and collaborating to defend its legitimate and natural interests.

The problem arises when those interests are conceived not as different but as antagonistic and irreconcilable with those of the other groups.

At this point, the group, as it happens to the individual as well, feels confronted by others, is afraid of them and, in short, experiences fear of freedom.

The solution, for the individual and the group, to this fear of freedom is **to change the concept of freedom** that generated that fear.

The only way to enjoy full freedom lies in replacing the traditional selfish concept of freedom by a supportive concept of freedom. It implies to consider the other individuals or groups as members of a larger group in which the vital interests of all can be reconciled.

This reconciliation requires a caring attitude, sensitive to the interests of others and an agreement on the rules of the game. These rules will be respected and considered correct and valid by everyone until another agreement is reached.

Nevertheless, **is a philosophy of solidarity compatible with the efficient functioning of an organization?**

Are the organizations designed, especially those operating in the market, just to compete with their rivals? Does competition necessarily imply an attitude of antagonism toward the others?

We must not be naive and ignore the social reality and the possible attacks that our competitors and even partners and collaborators could exercise against us. However, it is not realistic to say that the success of an organization requires the failure of others.

Something similar happens at a personal level. A person's success does not necessarily require the failure of others. In the future, Hobbes's concept will be abandoned and loyal cooperation will prove to generate more benefits than irreconcilable rivalry.

Excellence fully embraces the philosophy of cooperation within the organization, with outside organizations such as suppliers, and even with competitors. Cooperation does not require economic egalitarianism in wages. It can perfectly run in a context of different salaries and bonuses based on results but always with the requirement that the compensation rules are clear, accepted by all, and can be changed whenever a better option is found.

Applying the Excellence requires being convinced that the cooperation philosophy is correct. If management continues to believe that success is based on individualism, executive aggressiveness and the use of the levers of power, it is better to put aside the idea of implementing Excellence. It would be possible to opt for Product Quality or Quality Assurance but not for Excellence in Management.

12.3 How to motivate Quality Circles

The QCs should be rewarded fundamentally on an honorific way. The perception of economic incentives is often at odds with the spirit of collaboration that inspires TQM and can disrupt its implementation in the organization.

Often, individual merit pay systems prevent any possibility of teamwork. As noted by John Wooden[20] *"It's amazing what can be accomplished when nobody cares about who gets the credit".*

However, **exceptionally**, when the QC has given rise to a particular innovation in a product or process that has resulted in a very substantial profit increase, a monetary reward should be assigned to the QC team as a whole, letting the QC members to proceed to its internal distribution.

---

[20] John Wooden (1910-2010) Famous player and American basketball coach

When the improvements are progressive and happen little by little, it is not easy to quantify the reduction in costs or the increase in productivity due to them. In this case, a monetary reward can be given to the QC that originated them, without attempting to mathematically link it to the benefits derived from the improvements.

In any case, it is necessary **to think very carefully about the QCs economic rewards** and never set up incentives just because the employees are members of a QC.

It is counterproductive if employees perceive QCs as places where an additional wage premium can be earned, especially when the QCs operate, more or less, within the regular time schedule of the organization.

Anyway, leading or belonging to a QC and the quality of each member's participation **can and should be taken into account** in the process of employees' **promotions**.

In fact the QCs produce a **transformational** effect on their members; i.e., improve their values (commitment), attitudes (propensity to participation) and qualities (understanding of processes, communication, team management, knowledge, etc.).

These effects, similar to those produced by internal training, should be recognized and become part of the QCs members' **careers and professional promotions.**

The work of the QC members **can and should also be recognized** by explicit honorific attention, such as being congratulated by the management, invited to a dinner or celebration in their honor, etc.

12.4 QCs performance evaluation

Quality Circles do not generate suggestions continuously. Sometimes, they do not find solutions to the problems they have detected because, in many cases, the solutions may need to be found at a much higher level.

Yet members of the QCs should be **encouraged to address all** the problems detected and to invite other employees to do so, **avoiding** *"pointing the finger at anyone",* and suggesting, if possible, methods to avoid the same problems in the future.

It suffices to communicate these sugestions through a simple email to their respective bosses. If they are not competent to solve them, they must pass it on to a Unit manager or to the corresponding QC. If no solution is adopted, an explanation to why no action was taken should be given to the employee who pointed out the problem.

All communicated errors (and improvements) **are to be taken seriously**. Criticism of those who have the courage to point out what they consider a mistake or problem should not be tolerated. The TQM is always constructive and thankful for any collaboration, be it useful or not.

The QCs must control their own efficiency, especially the response delay and the adequacy of the measures they propose to solve the errors or problems that have been reported or detected.

The Quality Department, which is responsible for promoting Excellence and boosting the performance of QCs, must support their activities and **evaluate their performances** to encourage them to improve their own quality standard.

When we speak of assessment, there is a **simplistic tendency to center evaluation on the economic** profits obtained due to the costs reduction achieved by each QC in the processes or to the number of new successful designs that they have prepared.

The assessment of the QCs' activities centered in their direct contribution to the company profit has several weaknesses.

On the one hand, it is not easy, in many cases, to quantify the benefit increase that corresponds to the improvement. For example, to what extent the increase in sales has been the result of the introduction of certain improvements in the organization of the customer service. How can their effects be separated from the impact that the new ad campaign has had?

There may be small improvements that affect the main product of the company and therefore may lead to a large quantitative impact on the reduction of overall costs, while other improvements may have even a greater impact per unit of output, but because they affect a product of which fewer units are sold, they generate a lower overall cost reduction.

Which of these two improvements **is more important**? The one that generates greater economic benefit right now or another that is a lot more creative and may have an advantageous future impact?

Moreover, **it is unfair to think that QCs only add value to the extent that they reduce costs** in the processes. The QCs' mere existence consolidates a company culture focused on quality. This will have an impact on the company economic performance even if it is not immediate.

Therefore, Ishikawa considers that it is inadequate to evaluate the performance of a QC simply in terms of results, and points out that other criterions should be taken into consideration.

He suggests that the activity of the QCs should be evaluated according to the following factors:

Improvement Groups (QCs) Assesment, according to Ishikawa

Subjetc selection	20 puntos
Cooperative efforts	20 puntos
Understanding the context and the methods of analysis	30 puntos
Improvement findings	10 puntos
Standardization and avoiding Repetitions	10 puntos
Reconsidering the QC Procedures	10 puntos

Ishikawa attributes only a maximum of 10 points, from a total of 100, **to the results**, while **he gives priority** to other issues such as:
- The importance of the **subjects** that the QC has chosen for study (20 points)
- The amount of **effort** made by the QC (frequency and duration of meetings, number of attendees, participation of members of the QC, etc) (20 points)
- The **comprehension** of the methodology used for the analysis of the processes. This becomes evident when the QC applies techniques of analysis such: cause and effect diagram, histogram, check sheet, etc. If the QC applies these techniques, it becomes

more aware of the complexity of factors affecting quality. That implies a better knowledge of what quality is (30 points).
- The **achievements** obtained by standardizing and avoiding repetition in the **processes** (10 points)
- The overall effort of **rethinking and reflecting on** the functioning of the QC (10 points)

The evaluation method suggested by Ishikawa is inspired in a fundamental principle of TQM: *"If an adequate philosophy and technique of management is set up, good results will be achieved. If the organization is focused on achieving quality in their products, processes and own management system, it will eventually become a successful organization."*

12.5 Requirements for a successful QC

1. Sense of belonging to the QC. This happens when its members feel they are a team. QC membership should be voluntary. Nobody should be forced to participate in a QC. Each employee should feel free to choose the QC he prefers to join.

2. Commitment to the organization. The way the QCs operate should not harm the overall production process, and except for rare exceptions, it should not imply an extension of the working hours. The QCs functions must not enter in conflict with the objectives of the departments from which each of the QCs' members come to constitute the QC.

The QCs have the right to propose **revolutionary** changes in the work organization. Just only to propose, not to take decisions. **The rationale of all proposals** should be the accomplishment of the **mission** of the organization.

3. Well-defined purpose. The purpose of the QCs is to provide solutions for improvement. If they do not provide them within a reasonable period of time, they should then question their own permanence. The QCs should not serve as an excuse for employees to be absent from the production process. Its purpose is not to merely establish or develop relationships.

4. Appropriate members. It is highly desirable that the QCs include competent and productive people. The composition of the QCs, its interpersonal relationships and the way they work can deter highly capable employees from participating in them for fear of *"wasting their time"* or *"getting into personal conflicts".*

It is essential that the Department that coordinates the implementation and functioning of Excellence **supervises and gives support to the QCs**, in order to overcome the aforementioned obstacles and encourage the participation of valuable employees.

5. High Management supporting the QCs activities. It is a key factor for the success of a QC, especially at its early stages that the High Management, directly or by delegation:
 a) Shows, without a shadow of doubt, its will to implement and support TQM
 b) Clearly explains the philosophy of TQM
 c) Conducts training for teamwork, especially when the TQM is implemented in an organization not used to it
 d) Follows up the QCs functioning in a constructive way
 e) Reorients, where appropriate, the QCs functioning towards the fulfillment of its rationale: to provide solutions for improvement
 f) Receives suggestions from QCs and **answers** them rationally and in a short-term period, regardless if its response is favourable or not to the QCs proposals
 g) Recognizes the value of the efforts and results of the QCs.

13 THE ORGANIZATIONAL STRUCTURE FOR THE EXCELLENCE

Quality Circles or Improvement Groups, or whatever they may be called, are the basic cells for TQM.

If they do not exist, we cannot say that the Excellence has been adopted. We could say that the organization strongly stimulates improvement, innovation, reengineering, neotaylorism, studies of clients' needs, etc, but we cannot say that TQM is being implemented if QCs are not there.

Excellence requires constant, active, and voluntary employee participation. This participation will not take place if there is not a **proper channel** for it to happen continuously. **Suggestions' boxes** are not enough. The solution proposed by TQM is the **Quality Circles.** They can be different in terms of their numerical and qualitative composition and their field of action **but they must exist** as a participation channel.

An organ is required to encourage the creation of QCs, keep them running efficiently, and acknowledge their efforts and achievements.

This organ is none other than the **Quality Department** of the organization, which must be the disseminator of TQM philosophy throughout the organization as well as the assessing organ of the achievements in Excellence culture implementation and results.

The **Quality Department** must have the minimum number of staff members as possible.

As the number of Quality Circles grows, another position could appear in the organizational structure of Quality: the **Quality Coordinators**. These are also honorary positions. Usually, there is one Quality Coordinator **for every three or four** QCs.

Normally the Quality Coordinator is the president of one of these QCs -as elected by the presidents of the different QCs.

The Quality Coordinator's function is, on one hand, to communicate with the Quality Department, but without holding the monopoly over the communication, as any QC can place requests directly to the Quality Department, in case of an emergency or just to render communication easier.

On the other hand, QC Coordinators have the role of institutionalizing **communication between QCs** to promote the exchange of their experiences regarding the methods used, the achievements made, the lines of study initiated, etc.

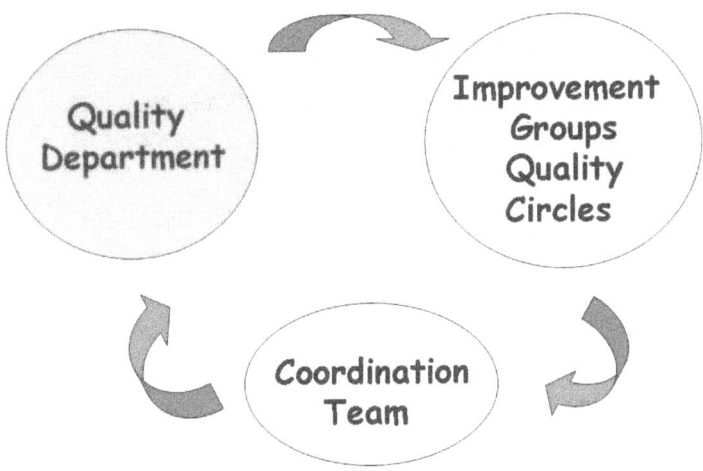

In small companies, the Quality Department may be formed by only one or two people who work part time to carry out the functions of the Quality Department in addition to their proper roles in the Units to which they belong.

However, no matter how small this Department may be, its existence is necessary to promote and coordinate the necessary actions for achieving the cultural change that Excellence requires.

In particular, the Quality Department has to assure ways to guarantee employee participation. Indeed, in most organizations there is real resistance to involve employees and ask their suggestions. Often *"participation"* is only encouraged as a formality.

There are many excuses to avoid the creation of this Quality Department:
- *"As we are just a handful of people, we are transparent; we do not need a Department of Quality"*
- *"The common employee does not have the capacity to participate actively"*
- *"It would be a waste of time"*
- *"It would be easier and more practical if their boss asked them directly for their opinion from time to time"*

The fact is that, in practice, most bosses **never find time to ask** for their employees' opinions; rarely do they ask their suggestions, and, in the end, the employee turns into some kind of machine that simply carries out just the task assigned to him and who keeps his creativity potential and ideas to himself.

In medium and large size companies, as in small ones, the same problems arise regarding the creation of the Quality Department. In those medium and large companies it is fully justified that some persons **devote their full-time** to making improvements and, in particular, promoting TQM.

In any case, the Quality Department **should have the fewest number** of members necessary. Only the needed persons to make it work (1 to 2 people)

The Quality Department must **avoid** the great mistake of acting bureaucratically.

Furthermore, the Quality Department must have a **clear authority** (hierarchical position) and be **linked directly to the Chairman** or the General-Director.
This is necessary to eliminate the risk of other Management Units paying little attention to the Quality Department because of its small size.
The Quality Department should be small but it should play a key role in the company.
The role of the Quality Department is mainly to promote Excellence and coordinate its implementation.

It is frequently believed that Excellence is a function that pertains only to the Quality Department. Some authors have suggested that Excellence should be a specialized expertise that resides in the Department of Total Quality.
Consequently, they argue that every effort associated with TQM should be managed by the staff of that Department. **That is also a very serious mistake.**
TQM **is not a concern exclusive** to the Quality Department.
The philosophy, methodology, and evaluation techniques of TQM should **never be a monopoly of the Quality Department**. Its obligation is to sow the TQM culture, disseminate it and make it

possible for the Head Management of the organization to then understand, discuss and use it.

The organization as a whole **should take ownership of** the Excellence/TQM working to its implementation and evaluation.

14 HOW TO IMPLEMENT EXCELLENCE

We will offer, hereinafter, a brief sequence of how to implement Excellence Management in an organization:

1. **Having a clear understanding** of the Excellence Philosophy: what it is, how it works, how to promote it.
The key point is to understand its essence.
Excellence is much more than a management technique. It is primarily a philosophy that uses techniques that are also partially used by other management philosophies.

2. Assuming that the Excellence is based on **FOUR essential Pillars**
Ignoring just one of them, would mean not be using the Excellence Management system.
These four pillars are:
- **Internal Clients** (staff and providers): they are the key factors to achieving Excellence. It is imperative that the human resources and the external collaborators of the organization become actively involved in the analysis, proposal, implementation and evaluation of improvements and innovations.
The Excellent organization must make them feel co-responsible and committed to the organization.

- **B. Spirit of Continuous Improvement**: The Excellent organization must constantly seek ways and areas in which to improve.

  The "absolute good" is never reached. Organizations, companies, technologies, etc. are dynamic. There will always be new goals to achieve, further improvements to introduce and new methods to apply. Excellence exists only if the organization has a spirit of continuous improvement.

- **C. Processes**: Every generation of products and services is achieved through processes.

  One of the main factors for improvement lies in reviewing and redesigning processes, and introducing new technologies and new forms of organization (yesterday, computers; today, self-telework and, who knows what other innovations will be introduced tomorrow).

  One of the most practical ways to improve processes is to search for good practices already existent through benchmarking.

  The Excellence Management strives to improve processes constantly.

- **D. External Clients/Customers**: Every organization must focus on its clients/customers.

The mission exists because there are clients to attend. Without clients, the existence of the organization has no point. Satisfying the customers is the purpose of the organization. The mission of the organization is not accomplished, or is not worthwhile, if its clients, whoever they are (government, enterprises, citizens) are not satisfied.

Moreover, the client is one of the most effective providers of suggestions that the organization can meet. Despising their potential contribution is walking towards a medium-term failure. Excellence requires that a special emphasis be placed on listening and receiving advice from the clients (which in addition is free).

3. Creating an Excellence Department

Any project must have a **driving center**. Sometimes, especially in medium and big-sized organizations, it is not easy for the managers to dedicate time to involve and reorganize the organization around the philosophy of Excellence.

The solution is to create a Department, as small as possible, whose mission is to spread and implement this philosophy in the organization. The manager of the organization should show unequivocal support to Excellence and to the Department of Excellence (Quality Department) which is in charge of orchestrating it practically.

4. Designing a Training Plan on Excellence

This Plan should explain and communicate what the purpose of Excellence is, what its philosophy is and how to implement this type of management.

Sometimes it is difficult for the managers to grasp the essence of Excellence philosophy. It is even more difficult for the employees to understand it, as they are not focused on management systems but on the execution of the tasks.

"Quality" seems very similar to *"clarity"*, and indeed, **when there is no clarity**, there is no quality. The key problem is that often the more basic and simple concepts are the most difficult to grasp.

Frequently, when people speak of quality they do not clarify what quality they are talking about: product-quality, process-quality or management-quality. As a result, this leads to great confusion in the training processes.

Furthermore, some quality experts wrongly identify TQM **with the methods** that assess whether the TQM is really being implemented. But, there **is no quality when there is no clarity.**

Designing a clear and concrete training plan is a key factor to convey the new management philosophy to the organization. In addition, TQM requires new forms of participation and involvement. Therefore, it is also very important to organize training sessions in specific techniques, such as collecting and analyzing suggestions, teamwork skills, technical evaluation of improvements, organizational culture, etc.

Ishikawa underlines that for the TQM to penetrate the organizational culture, every employee must attend one or two courses on Excellence. He also considers that it is necessary a period of approximately 10 years for the Excellence training to completely settle down and become integrated in the organization culture.

However, its positive results begin to be perceived right from the first year of its implementation. Nowadays we consider that the implementation and cultural change can be much faster if the necessary will and means are there. (Indeed, not many and not too expensive means are needed to train in Excellence).

5. Creating Quality Circles

Employee participation must be implemented and promoted. Quality Circles are the organs where most of the concrete proposals to improve processes and products should arise. If an organization does not have Quality Circles, or Improvement Groups, it is not possible to qualify it as Excellent.

6. Establishing an action **schedule**

The philosophy of Total Quality is not at odds with the practice. There is nothing more practical, from an organizational point of view, than **to establish a timetable** of actions to do; a schedule flexible and reviewable that reflects the responsibilities and commitments assumed by the organization. It should include the Quality Costs studies, Benchmarking data collection, Improvement proposals and so on.

7. Quickly **debugging and assessing** the QCs proposals

Keeping the QCs alive requires recognizing the potential value of their performance. It is necessary that the Management be agile and swift and answers to the specific QCs proposals.

The proposals are not to be accepted just because they are brought up by the QCs. However, not to respond to their proposals promptly and quickly, even when the proposals are turned down, shows that the organization does not recognize the essential role that the TQM assigns to them.

8. Implementing the proposals that are deemed appropriate

Recognizing the value of a feasible contribution is worth very little if it is not put into practice. Successful proposals ought to be implemented, unless there are clear reasons not to do so, such as lack of resources or the need for a high level of additional investment.

9. Evaluating the results of the implementation of accepted proposals

The effects of the improvements can be seen after their maturing process. As well as for the implementation, it is very convenient to be supported by the QCs at this assessing stage. The QCs themselves can be the ones to do the evaluation, or maybe a different QC from the one that made the proposal. In any case, the evaluation should be done in a realistic and constructive way, reasoned and public, focusing on recognizing and learning from the experience.

10. **Going back through the nine previous stages at a higher level**, (in **others areas** of the organization) **or doing** a thorough analysis in order to tackle improvement more radically.

15 IMPLEMENTING EXCELLENCE: MOST FREQUENT MISTAKES

The expectations about the Excellence Management often fade away when it comes to implementing it. This is due to multiple errors in the design or implementation of Excellence. Among the **main common mistakes,** it is worth noting the following:

1. Ignoring the internal client

One of the most difficult aspects of any management is to involve those employees who are willing to be involved in the creative process.

The main obstacle to this action is the **diehard leadership**, the assumption that people are not going to collaborate and that it will require too much time for them to do so, or that their contributions will be of little value.

Then, the initial choice of Excellence is often reduced to a more or less modernized version of the old Taylorist approach. That is, changing the type of management is indeed limited to the creation of a Department of Organization and Methods, which proposes and develops improvements.

If that happens, the Excellence Management **is soon forgotten**. In this case, employees would not be considered a key source of suggestions and, at best, they would simply have the mere option of submitting their ideas via a Suggestion Box.

2. Trying to apply the Excellence Management **right from the start in all areas** of activity of the organization

The implementation of TQM **should be done little by little**. At the beginning, it is enough to focus just on some of the main important activities of the organization.

One of the main reasons for the success of the Efficiency Unit for the Improvement of Public Administration in Britain, during the governments of Margaret Thatcher in the 80's, was to achieve specific improvements, even in secondary activities, **which could serve as example to encourage** improvements in other activities of the organization.

Derek Rayner, director of the Efficiency Unit, allowed each Ministry to decide the areas for improvement in activities or Directorates that they considered the most appropriate.

Subsequently, as an imitative effect, an analytical and improving process was put into action **in the rest** of the activities of other Directorates and Units of each Ministry.

Therefore, it is necessary to avoid the mistake of trying to bring Excellence to all areas of the organization right from the very beginning. It is better to concentrate efforts and to get good results in some areas and then to extend this new management style to the rest of Units of the organization.

3. Requiring absolute perfection from the very first moment

We should not expect to reach absolute perfection right away but to create a self-improvement dynamic. *"Se hace el camino al andar"* (The path is paved by walking) as Antonio Machado, a Spanish poet, said. Improvement is always possible.

Implementing Excellence does not mean that the whole organization, in all its units, activities and processes, will run flawlessly from the first day.

The processes implantation and the spirit of improvement need time to consolidate in all activities of the organization.

4. Creating **processes** whose only objective is to **control the employees**

All processes must be conceived as a means to facilitate activities, including their own self-control, but **not only as mechanisms to control from outside** what is happening inside.

The employees should not view the processes as a Big Brother who controls all their movements, **but as a help** that allows them to fulfill their mission with most ease and assurance of effectiveness.

Excellence does not deny the usefulness of control checklists. For example, it is necessary that airline pilots check all indicators prior to the take-off. It is also convenient that those in charge of the cleanliness of a hotel room follow guidelines for cleaning and replacing equipment to ensure that the room has been properly prepared.

However, it is necessary **to avoid the mistake** of thinking that the essence of Excellence lies in the mere mechanical or bureaucratic methodology of control or execution.

Employees, at all levels, need to feel encouraged to propose improvements in the processes with the scope to facilitate their work and improve the achievement of the final product or service. It is necessary that they consider the processes as theirs and even the organization as their own. This will not happen if the employees consider the processes just as a mean to control their activities.

5. **Falling** into the temptation of looking for **someone to blame**

It is very common, within the organizations, to look for someone to blame for the errors committed. **This attitude is totally contrary to the Excellence Philosophy**. It is necessary to always have a constructive spirit. The past is the past. Now is the time for improving.

We must not look for the ones to blame. It is not the important thing to do. Let us look for solutions. Excellence points out that we must **not focus on identifying *"the one to blame"*** but rather on thanking and congratulating the people on their efforts and success.

16 ASSESSING WHETHER EXCELLENCE IS REALLY BEING APPLIED

All management and administrative philosophies and techniques will only produce results if managers (leaders) support and implement them.

Eventually the managers will face a challenge: to get the most from that philosophy, and make sure that its implementation is being optimized.

A simple way of evaluating how effective the manager of a company is could be by having a look at the company results statements.

Nevertheless, bad results in a given year could have been accompanied by an effective job of reviewing production processes, whose good effects **would be only felt** in the following years.

Similarly, if the management style has improved the level of staff satisfaction in a particular year, this can probably **lead to higher** motivation and better results **in the future**. Investing in the development of the skills of the staff can be also translated into higher productivity later on.

In sum, the evaluation of the manager of an organization should be viewed in terms of their performance in different fields:
- Leadership style
- Planning
- Human resources development
- Process designing
- Efficiency in the use of any type of resources
- Results on client satisfaction,
- Results on Human resources satisfaction
- Results on Profit
- Etc.

The assessment should not only consider the short-term results but also the results in terms of strengthening and building the capacity of the organization.

The evaluation should be done not just punctually but **over a period.**

Excellency is a philosophy and a way of managing organizations that embraces the principles of **continuous improvement.**

This should be also reflected in the results:
- How to evaluate what has been improved?
- How to evaluate if there are areas where the opportunities for improvement are higher?
- How to evaluate the results?

Any evaluation requires a methodology that lays out **what** to assess and **how** to do it.

16.1 The EFQM model. Its origins

In 1988, fourteen leading European companies took the initiative to establish an institution (the European Foundation for Quality Management EFQM) to help the European organizations to improve their performance.

The EFQM **took, as a reference, other existent methodologies** such as Deming Prizes in **Japan** and Baldrige Awards in **USA**.

Then, the EFQM built a new model to assess how close an organization is to Excellence. The EFQM model has great similarities to those used in Japan and USA.

Indeed, nowadays the **Excellence models are very similar worldwide**, even when they differ in the number of assessment criterions used.

All models expect the same: to assess the degree in which the company has implemented the philosophy of Excellence and the attitudes and behaviors that this philosophy implies.

In 1991, the EFQM established the European Quality Award and offered its assessment model to the companies and organizations that wanted to use it for self-assessment and/or to compete for the European Quality Award.

The EFQM model evaluates which companies and organizations are properly applying the actions arising from the philosophy of Excellence, indicating to what extent they are close to Excellence in Management.

The EFQM model was designed to be used **by the organization itself**.

Usually, the companies keep their own accounts and interpret them; generating accounting reports (statement of profit and loss, assets balance sheet, assets and related accounts).

Similarly, the organization itself is the one to understand, assimilate and apply the EFQM model in a process called **self-assessment,** and does not need to rely on external consultants.

Initially, it may be convenient to count on **outside expertise** in order to get a better understanding of the factors pointed by the model and how to evaluate them, but this is not essential to start applying the model.

However, the support of an institution of assessment such as the European Foundation for Quality Management, or any other, is useful to confirm the correctness of the evaluation made and to facilitate the exchange of experiences with other organizations that are using the same model (EFQM).

16.2 EFQM contents

Good management may not produce good results immediately and, similarly, good results can be fortuitous and not due to good management. However, when good management is applied continuously, good results will start to show.

The European Excellence Model (EFQM) is a model that serves to evaluate the most significant parameters of an organization to indicate which of them can be improved and to what extent.

The EFQM model takes into account **nine criterions** that are considered representative of the key fields of a good management. It allows an X-ray of the way the organization is being managed. The original nine criterions **have changed slightly** since 1991, but its original core remains.

The EFQM has also an assessment **methodology** in which, over time, formal modifications have been introduced, but not in its essence.

The scoring structure has also evolved but this is not the essence of the system.

Indeed, the philosophies of both Parmenides and Heraclitus can be applied to the EFQM Excellence model.

Parmenides, because the essence of the model (the original nine criterions and the assessment methodology) remains.

Heraclitus, because the model has included changes over time, in the contents of the criteria, in evaluation systems (questionnaire, formulary) and in the scores assigned to different criteria and sub-criteria.

The model has experienced **successive versions** in 2006, 2010 and 2013 that have not changed its essence. We emphasize once again that the model should be an encouragement and incentive for improvement through a self-evaluation process. The model should not be something to pursue **but to be used** by the organizations. That would be Deming's way of thinking.

However, it is **understandable** that some organizations may wish to obtain a certification that validates the score they have given themselves. This gives them the confidence that they have assessed themselves well.

It is also understandable that they wish to hold a public recognition and even to apply for a stamp or prize of Excellence.

However, Deming would say that that is secondary and what really matters is the improvement achieved. This is what really gives the market the authentic image of the company. Always remember that the model is a tool (a mean) but the target (the objective) should be to implement excellence.

16.2.1 EFQM nine criteria

As previously stated, the original nine criterions have changed slightly since 1991. For example, the initial criterion Policy and Strategy has become Strategy, the criterion Resources has become Partnerships and Resources, and the criterion Processes has become Processes, Products and Services.

Five of these criterions assess the management carried out by an organization on its key **Productive Resources** (Leadership, Strategy, Staff, Partnership and Resources, and Processes, Products and Services).

The remaining **four** criterions evaluate the **achieved Results** (Client Satisfaction, Staff Satisfaction, Results on Society and Business Results).

In the following pages we are going to present the main ideas of the EFQM 2013 model criterions. Nevertheless, we would like to invite the readers to go directly to EFQM publications if they want a more updated and thorough study.

As the reader will see, the criterions concentrate de main ideas that have been presented in the previous pages regarding the Total Quality philosophy.

1. Leadership

The leader, or manager, has a decisive role in the implementation and development of Excellence.

This criterion assesses the extent to which the management team of the organization encourages, supports and promotes a culture of TQM.

It does not assess whether the manager is good or bad, since there may be extraordinary managers from the perspective of a Taylorist approach or other management conceptions.

Its aim is **to assess the extent to which the behavior** and actions of the management team **are consistent with the TQM philosophy** and, in particular, the extent to which it instills and promotes the adoption of this philosophy at all levels of the organization.

Excellent organizations have leaders who shape the future and "make it happen", acting as models of their values and ethics, and inspiring trust at all times. They are flexible, enabling the organization to anticipate and react in a timely manner to ensure the on-going success of the organization.

To evaluate this aspect, questions such as the following should be asked:
- Does the leader show interest in listening to clients and providers?
- Does he recognize and thank the efforts made by the staff?
- Does he promote staff training in Excellency?
- Does he show support for TQM in front of other organizations?
- Etc.

The evaluation of the criterion Leadership consists in evaluating the following sub-criteria:
- 1a. Leaders develop the mission, values and ethics and act as role models.
- 1b. Leaders define, monitor and review and drive the improvement of the organization's management system and performance.
- 1c. Leaders engage with external stakeholders
- 1d. Leaders reinforce a culture of excellence with the organization's people.
- 1e. Leaders ensure that the organization is flexible and manage change effectively.

2. Strategy

The actions and statements of the management will promote Excellence if the Strategy of the organization is built under a wide and participative approach.

Reciprocally, the agreed strategy must be the inspiring and guiding axis of the leaders' actions.

The evaluation of this criterion aims to show the extent to which the management considers TQM as a core element of the Policy and Strategy of the organization; it also evaluates how well **its principles are reflected** in the design, elaboration, development and revision of the Strategy document of the organization.

To assess this criterion, questions such as the following should be asked:
- Does the organization have a defined Strategy in which TQM is advocated?
- Is the Strategy developed following the principles of Excellence?
- Who takes part in this process?
- Are the participants given real participative roles in agreement with the TQM principles?
- What information and what considerations were taken into account?
- Have the customers, suppliers and employees been consulted regarding the Strategy?

- How is the Strategy communicated to the staff?
- Via meetings, circulars, web page, etc?
- Is the Strategy revised?
- Are suggestions welcome?
- From whom?
- Etc.

The evaluation of the criterion Strategy consists in evaluating the following sub-criteria:

- 2a. Strategy is based on understanding the needs & expectations of both stakeholders and the external environment.
- 2b. Strategy is based on understanding internal performance & capabilities.
- 2c. Strategy and supporting policies are developed, reviewed and updated.
- 2d. Strategy and supporting policies are communicated, implemented and monitored

3. Staff management

This criterion aims to measure the extent to which the organization uses the full potential of its human resources, the way in which staff capacities are being developed, how the staff is involved, how their efforts are recognized, etc.

The importance that the TQM attributes to the employee, as its Internal Client, must be manifested in the style of management, development and use of the human resources potential.

To assess this criterion, questions such as the following should be asked:
- How is the optimal performance of employees stimulated?
- Are the objectives of the staff set up and their performances reviewed regularly, having into account their opinions?
- Are staff skills maintained and developed?
- What kind of recognition is used?
- Are the work teams or the Quality Circles promoted?
- Is there any training action regarding teamwork?
- How is the staff participation promoted in the organization?
- Is there an effective dialogue with the staff regarding all staff management aspects?
- Is communication actually encouraged?
- Is the development of each employee's talent encouraged?
- Etc

The evaluation of the criterion Staff Management consists in evaluating the following sub-criteria:

- 3a. Staff's plans support the organization's strategy
- 3b. Staff's knowledge and capabilities are developed.
- 3c. Staff is aligned, involved and empowered.
- 3d. Staff communicates effectively throughout the organization.
- 3e. Staff is rewarded, recognized and cared for.

4. Partnerships and Resources (Material, Technology and others)

This criterion evaluates the way in which the organization manages its material resources, the extent to which it uses the potential offered by the economic and financial resources, information and technological resources, its infrastructures, etc. and its Partnerships.

To asses this criterion questions as the following should be asked:
- Are the potential allies and providers identified?
- Has the organization developed constructive relations with them?

- Is cash flow well used?
- Are non-quality costs calculated?
- Are there any agile systems of information exchange inside the company?
- Is it complicated for the Units to access to information, confidential or non- confidential, that other departments have?
- Is the whole potential of information being used and communicated to the scientific community or offered as a product, priced or not, to the people interested in it?
- Are the stock departments well managed?
- Are there any studies about the possibilities for improvement of the delivery and deposit system?
- Is the use of facilities, reunion halls, and premises optimized?
- Are the available technological means used in a proper way?
- Is the intellectual property of this technology protected?
- Is it being offered as an organization product?
- Are new products and services offered?
- Etc

The evaluation of the criterion Partnership and Resources Management consists in evaluating the following sub-criteria:

- 4a. Partners and suppliers are managed for sustainable benefit.
- 4b. Finances are managed to secure sustained success
- 4c. Buildings, equipment, materials and natural resources are managed in a sustainable way.
- 4d. Technology is managed to support the delivery of strategy.
- 4e. Information and knowledge are managed to support effective decision making and to build the organization's capability

5. Processes, Products and Services

Every organization must accomplish its mission, generating products or services through processes.

Excellence emphasizes that poor design of processes is the most significant cause of failures in the products, much more than the employee's carelessness or ill will. Therefore, an essential criterion for the success of an organization lies in the importance it attaches to reviewing and improving processes.

The criterion evaluates the way in which the organization identifies, manages, verifies and improves its processes, products and services.

This must be done through TQM philosophy, which is very different from Taylor's theory. As an example, we must point out the fact that Taylor himself would get a score on this criterion far from the maximum possible because he does not give importance to the suggestions coming from the employees (internal clients) or from the external clients.

The evaluation of this criterion implies answers to questions[21] such as:
- Have the key processes of the company in different areas of activity been listed?
- Are they described in detail?
- Are there any production standards in every phase of the processes?
- Are evaluations being done in every phase of the processes?
- Does the management reflect upon these evaluations?
- How many processes do the Quality Circles act upon?
- Are there any systems to collect suggestions about the way in which the processes could be improved?
- Do these suggestions, opinions and systems work well?

---

[21] Nowadays, the criterion also includes to assess whether the products and services are developed, promoted and efficiently produced, and whether there are good relations with the clients. Consecuently, questions are asked about these issues.

- Are the suggestions revised?
- Are the systems to collect suggestions revised?
- Have modifications been introduced in the processes?
- Does the management inform about the changes to be introduced in the processes and the reasons for these changes?
- Are the opinions about these changes admitted?
- Has the organization developed its products and services?
- Are the products and services reviewed and updated?
- Are innovation and creativity encouraged
- Are they adequately promoted and disseminated?
- Are they produced effectively?
- To what extent emphasis is placed on the customer side?
- Etc.

The evaluation of the criterion Processes, Products and Services consists in evaluating the following sub-criteria:
- 5a. Processes are designed and managed to optimize stakeholder value.
- 5b. Products and services are developed to create optimum value for customers.

- 5c. Products and services are effectively promoted and marketed
- 5d. Products and services are produced, delivered and managed.
- 5e. Customer relationships are managed and enhanced.

6. Clients' satisfaction

Within TQM, the concept of client is fundamental. This criterion measures the satisfaction of the external clients, be them citizens, enterprises or public institutions.

Client satisfaction is a guarantee for the future stability of the organization, either because it implies that it has captured a market share or because it has produced services (health, justice, education, legislation, etc.) which are considered valuable by the clients, justifying the continuation of the organization.

Questions as the following should be asked:
- Are you satisfied with the products and services?
- Which of them is most successful?
- Are you satisfied with the treatment received?
- Are you satisfied with the prices?
- Does the maintenance assistance work well?

- Does the system of complaints and claims work well?
- Are the clients encouraged to make suggestions?
- Does the organization thank them for their suggestions?
- Etc.

The evaluation of Clients' Satisfaction through their **direct** or **indirect** opinions is a key indicator of the performance of the organization. The evaluation of this criterion consists in evaluating the following sub-criteria:

- 6a. Direct assessment of clients' **perception.**

These are the customer's perceptions of the organization. These perceptions should give a clear understanding of the effectiveness, from the customer's perspective, of the deployment and outcomes of the organization's customer strategy and supporting policies and processes

- 6b. **Performance** indicators.

These are the internal measures used by the organization in order to monitor, understand, predict and improve the performance of the organization and to predict their impact on the perceptions of its customers.

These indicators should give a clear understanding of the deployment and impact of the organization's customer strategy, supporting policies and processes.

Indirect assessment of clients' satisfaction through their behavior (fidelity), and the opinion of specialized magazines, etc.

7. Staff satisfaction

According to Excellence, the staff is an internal client. Therefore, the assessment of staff satisfaction is a very important indicator of their level of motivation and commitment to the organization.

Employee loyalty, availability and interest are assets for the stability and dynamism of the organization and therefore for its future and its ability to produce value.

The surveys about staff satisfaction, carried out under circumstances of total freedom (full guarantee of anonymity, precise and comprehensive questions, etc.) are crucial in order to assess their degree of satisfaction.

This requires asking questions such as:
- Are you satisfied with the work climate?
- Is the work environment good in your department?
- Are you satisfied with the leadership style?
- Is the reward system fair?
- Do you share the values of the organization?

- Are there any adequate participation channels?
- Do you consider that the possibilities for professional promotion are fair?
- What is the degree of certainty with respect to your job?
- Are there any professional training possibilities offered to you?
- Can you really offer suggestions and opinions?
- Does the leadership collect the employees' opinions?
- Etc.

Apart from the answers offered by the staff, it is important to take into consideration objective data such as: the degree of absenteeism, staff migration to other organizations, the level of participation in the improvement teams or Quality Circles, etc.

These data assesses the employees' desire to remain in the organization and their level of commitment.

The evaluation of Staffs' Satisfaction is a key indicator of the capacity building of the organization.

The evaluation of this criterion consists in evaluating the following sub-criteria:

- 7a. Perceptions

These are the staff, managers and employees' perceptions of the organization on topics such as: Satisfaction, involvement and commitment; motivation and delegation and accountability; assessment of leadership and management; assessment of management skills, talent and performance; training, recognition and career development; existence of a real and effective communication; working conditions, etc.

These perceptions should give a clear understanding of the **effectiveness**, from the staff's perspective, of the deployment and outcomes of the organization's strategy and supporting policies and processes.

- 7b. Performance indicators

These are the internal measures used by the organization in order to monitor, understand, predict and improve the performance of the organization's staff and to predict their impact on perceptions

They must measure aspects such as activities of involvement and commitment; management activities of competence and performance; training activities, recognition and career development; internal communication, etc.

8. Impact upon Society

Excellence supports a global vision, both in time and in space.

That is why it cares not only for a short-term horizon but also for medium or long-term ones. It is also concerned not only about the direct clients but also about the impact that the organization has **upon the social environment**.

The more the organization generates a positive impact on its environment, the better the perception about the organization image is.

That is why it is logical to consider, as an achievement of the organization, everything attained in terms of satisfying the needs and expectancies of the local, national and international community; although this is not part of the specific mission of the organization.

This criterion also includes the evaluation of the organization impact or influence on the quality of life and on the preservation of natural resources.

The evaluation of this criterion implies taking into consideration the opinions of the public institutions, mass media, professionals, trade unions, political organizations, etc.

The assessment is done through questions such as the following:
- Do they believe that our organization has a positive role in society?

- Does it generate direct and indirect jobs?
- Are its production processes detrimental to the environment?
- Does it care for the aesthetics of the environment?
- Does it collaborate with or get involved in social and sports events, charity activities, receptions, etc?
- How does society perceive the way in which the organization cares for the quality of life, the environment cleanliness and the preservation of natural resources?
- How does the organization relate and works with the authorities that regulate the organization activities?
- Etc.

The evaluation of Impact upon Society is, more and more, an important indicator of the excellence of the organization.

The evaluation of this criterion consists in evaluating the following sub-criteria:

- 8a. Perceptions

These perceptions should give a clear understanding of the effectiveness, from society's perspective, of the deployment and outcomes of the organization's social and environmental strategy in aspects such as environmental impact; the impact on society (employment, presence, etc.).

It can be measured through the media coverage, the prizes granted to the social activities of the organization, etc.

- 8b. Performance indicators

These are the internal measures used by the organization in order to monitor, understand, predict and improve the performance of the organization and to predict their impact on the perceptions of the relevant stakeholder within society.

They must measure aspects such as its economic and employment impact; its environmental and social activities; its compliance with the legislation and the different government regulations; its results regarding health and safety; its socially responsible management of purchases and suppliers, etc.

9. Business or Key results

Economic and production indicators are crucial to evaluate any company or organization. They reflect the accomplishment of the core mission of the organization.

This criterion seeks to assess what has been achieved in relation to the planned business goals: production rates, profit rates, cost reductions, business activities development and enlargement, etc.

In public organizations that do not operate in the market, it is more difficult to assess this component of the results. Nevertheless, there is always a way to do it: taking into account the output, regardless of the economic costs which that output has implied; comparing the standard costs with those of other organizations; analyzing the cost per product in relation to previous years, etc.

It means, in short, to assess the achievements that have being attained in relation to the planned business objectives as well as the degree of satisfaction of the needs and expectations of all those who have an interest, economic or otherwise, in the organization.

The assessment is done through questions such as the following:

- What benefit has been obtained in the current financial year?
- How has profit evolved from previous years?
- What is the increase in the value of the organization assets?
- How has its value evolved in the market or Stock Exchange?
- Has the production costs per unit of output been reduced?
- Has the production capacity increased?

- How has the number of faulty products evolved?
- Etc.

The evaluation of this criterion consists in evaluating the following sub-criteria:

- 9a. Business outcomes

These are the key economic and non-economic business outcomes which demonstrate the success of the organization's deployment of their strategy.

Measures such as: economic results; the perceptions of the interest groups that provide funding; the results of management and budget control; the volume of products or public services; the results of key processes, etc

- 9b. Business performance indicators

These are the key financial and non-economic business indicators that are used to measure the organization's **operational** performance. They help to monitor, understand, predict and improve the organization's likely business outcomes.

Measures such as: costs of plans, programs and projects; unit costs by product type; performance of key processes; the performance of partners and suppliers; the development of technology, information and knowledge, etc.

16.2.2 The PDCA cycle

The EFQM model uses an assessment approach based on Deming's PDCA cycle (Plan-Do-Check-Act). It is a strategy of quality continuous improvement in four steps, based on a system devised by Walter A. Shewhart.

In essence, it comes to assess whether the management has been realized:

a. **Thinking beforehand** about what the manager expects from each mean of production (leadership, strategy, staff, material, financial and technological resources, processes, etc). In other words, having a good approach, that is, having a clear understanding of what each mean must contribute to the production.

b. **Launching each mean.** That is, going from plan to action.

c. **Reviewing how everything has worked** to see if there have been differences from what had been planned. Assessing and learning from it and adopting, if needed, new approaches to be implemented.

d. **Implementing** the conclusions learned; implementing the new approaches.

For example, in the case of Staff Management, it would be **necessary to check if** there are evidences that **the manager:**
- **Has thought** about how they are going to be trained, how they will be involved in the actions, how the collection of their opinions will be done, etc.
- **Has acted**, organizing their training, motivating them, gathering their opinions, etc.
- **Has assessed** whether the training plan has been realized, if it has been helpful; if the staff is motivated, if their views have been collected, if they have provided useful ideas, etc. and drawn conclusions from all this.
- **Has implemented** actions depending on what has been learned from the findings.

The EFQM applies the PDCA, which it calls the logic RADAR (**R**esults, **A**pproach, **D**eployment, **A**ssessment and **R**eview) to review and evaluate the actions focused under each sub-criterion.

Thus, it aims to detect the strong and also the weak points. These last ones are called, with a positive approach, Areas for Improvement in order to avoid negative connotations, because actually any weakness detected is an Area for potential Improvement.

According to the RADAR logic, every organization needs to:

- Establish the **R**esults it wants to achieve as part of its strategy
- Plan and schedule a series of solidly grounded and integrated **A**pproaches that lead the organization to the required results.
- **D**eploy the approaches in a systematic way to ensure its implementation.
- **A**ssess, **R**eview and perfect the deployed approaches by monitoring and analyzing the results achieved and the ongoing learning activities.

This guideline should be applied in each sub-criterion in order to check whether the PDCA cycle is being applied and then assess it, taking into account the founded evidences.

The EFQM model applies to the Management of Enablers (the first five criteria) the PDCA (RADAR) methodology using the following terminology:

a) For **phase Plan,** the EFQM uses the term **Approach**, which means the degree of understanding we have of each sub-criterion and therefore our capacity to apply it adequately.
b) Then for **phase Do**, the term **Deployment** is used, that is, the way the theoretical approach is put into practice, checking if it has been applied in all or only in some areas of the organization

c) Then for **phase Check** the EFQM uses the term **Measurement**, which means to verify the effectiveness of the theoretical approaches and their subsequent deployment.
d) Finally to the **phase Act,** the EFQM uses the terms **Learning and Creativity** to assess whether the organization has used its approach, deployment and measurement, to draw conclusions that can be translated into **improvement ideas** to be implemented in the organization.

In the next cycle, the Approach will be enhanced with those learnings, which will need to be Deployed, and their effectiveness Measured, giving room to new Learning and new ideas for improvement, nourishing the continuous improvement process which by definition never ends.

The EFQM model also applies the PDCA (RADAR) methodology to analyze the **Results** as it enquires if the **right objectives were planned**, if they were **actually sought**, if it was **verified** what was produced and its **adequacy** to the previously planned objectives and if the leadership has **learned anything** to redefine the plan of objectives for the next cycle

This should be done with **every type of results** (Clients, People, Society and Key results):

e) Checking if they are a **coherent set of results**, taking into account the mission of the organization; if they meet the needs and expectations of relevant stakeholders, and if they fit with the strategy and objectives.

f) Checking whether the results have been **timely, reliable, accurate and proper** to each customer's segment. This process should lead to an in-depth knowledge of the achievements of the organization, in order to, if necessary, redefine future results to be obtained.

g) Measuring the results to see if they have a **positive trend** or not to observe if the results are achieved on an **ongoing** basis, according to the **strategic** objectives.

h) Making relevant **external comparisons** to learn from other organizations. Assessing whether there is founded trust in that the performance levels will be maintained in the future.

Taking the PDCA cycle as an axis allows the companies to enter into a dynamic of comprehensive improvement of products, services, processes and procedures, reducing costs, optimizing productivity, reducing prices, increasing and strengthening their market share and increasing competitiveness and profitability.

This continuous improvement approach **can sometimes become obsessive or tiring** for the managers, whose main concern is the daily management of the organization, and for the units that are focused on producing. This pressure **should be mitigated** by the use of common sense in the process of continuous improvement.

The worst that could happen is that the managers, or the units, see Total Quality as an enemy, instead of a collaborator. If this happened and a climate of mistrust had been generated, it would be necessary to replace the head of the Quality Department for his inability to create a culture of excellence in the company.

Excellence **involves the production units** in the process of creation and improvement. This is a different approach from Taylor's who considered that the traditional units of Organization and Methods should be the ones in charge of the improvement processes.

However, how is it possible for the productive units to harmonize the daily demands of management and production with its contribution to creativity and continuous improvement?

The tension that derives from it may lead to a tendency to delegate to the Quality Department the full responsibility for the development of continuous improvement and, consequently, to give to it a certain authority over the production units.

To avoid conflicts between the Department of Excellence and the production units, it is suggested:

a) **To delegate** to the Excellence Department **the prompting** of the improvement, not its development. The development must come primarily from producing units themselves.

b) To empower the Quality Department with a role that emphasizes **cooperation**, without any hierarchical connotation and that involves a clear understanding of the burden the productive units have daily.

c) To reiterate frequently that **creativity** is the result of a set of a reasonable **involvement and participation** of all units.

16.2.3 The scoring system

Any assessment needs to be expressed in quantitative terms even when what it measures are aspects whose quantification depends on the subjective opinion of the evaluator.

This is the case of most evaluations made in social life. Any assessment involves subjective judgment regardless if it is about the beauty of a painting, the suitability of a public work project, the potential of a person as director or the choice of the horse winner in an exhibition.

It is only possible to make objective assessments in the fields of chemical and physical quantities, for example, on issues such as size, distance, weight, temperature, thickness, density, wave-length, etc.

However, to avoid that subjectivity lead to arbitrary decisions with little foundation, it is usual to establish some criteria, which constitute the framework of opinion for the evaluation.

Each criterion is given a maximum of points, which are distributed among the various sub-criteria that have been established for each criterion. This assessment framework helps to put in objective terms the subjectivity of the evaluator. The more accurate the definition of each criterion and sub-criterion is, the more reinforced the objectivity is.

In the EFQM model, both the criteria selected and the points assigned to each of them were the results of reflections made during the work to define the model.

The model allows a maximum score of 1000 points, of which 500 are to assess the **management** of the means of production that make the organization work and the other 500 to assess the **results** obtained.

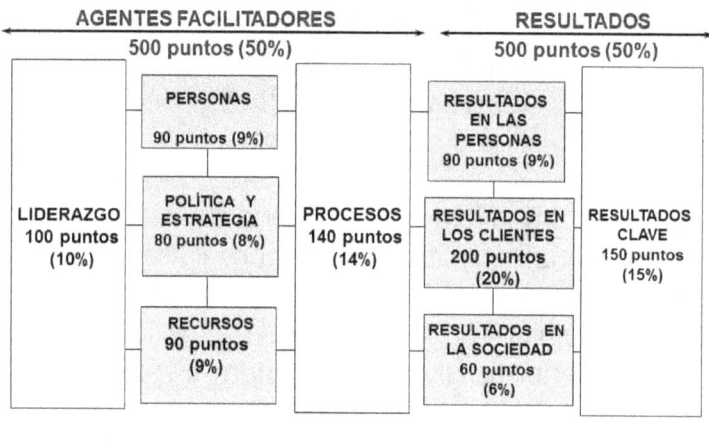

Originally, the EFQM attributed a different number of points to each criterion: Leadership 100, Strategy and Policy 80, Staff Management 90, Other Resources Management 90, Processes 140, Client

Satisfaction 200, Staff Satisfaction 90, Impact on Society 60 and Key Results 150.

Nowadays, the model has changed its structure of points and assigns 100 points to every criterion, except to Key Results and Client Satisfaction, assigning to each 150 points.

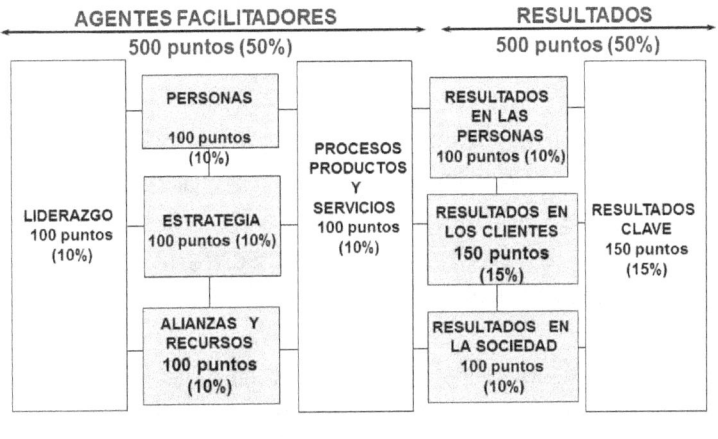

However, as I stress in my courses, **the distribution of points is not the key part** of the model. The fundamental part is the nine criteria and, above all, the philosophy of excellence that lies behind.

What any excellent Executive should look for is that his organization achieves the **maximum score in each criterion,** regardless if the EFQM assigned to it a score of 80 points in 2000, or a 100 points in 2013.

Obviously the points must be taken into account if it is to compete for a prize or for an EFQM Certification that accredit the score attained.

Moreover, even in the best companies, the highest scores achieved are often far from 1000 points. Excellence points to a horizon and suggests that there is always margin for further improvement.

The EFQM model, like any evaluation methodology (eg, methods HAY, Bedaux, of job evaluation) requires that the evaluator, above all, has **a clear understanding** of the principles underlying the model; then an adequate **knowledge** of the criteria and sub-criteria and, finally, **expertise** in evaluation.

Within the general framework of the EFQM model specific assessment methodologies were then defined, taking into account the different contexts such as: Small, Medium and Large Enterprise; Public or Private Sector; Educational, Sanitary Institutions, etc. The idea was to adapt the questionnaires to the peculiarities of the different groups.

In that line it is likely that any organization, which depends on various offices or similar units, set for each sub-criterion of EFQM lines of interpretation, or simplified and specific questionnaires, to facilitate and standardize the self-assessments carried out by its various offices and units.

The purpose of existing methodologies should be **to facilitate the task** of both internal and external evaluators, guiding them in detail and with examples on how to assess each sub-criterion.

The EFQM model is **not a goal in itself but a means** through which to assess excellence. Like any other assessment model, it is not a sacred model. What is important is how useful it is to promote excellence.

One of the greatest threats to excellence is its bureaucratization. Even with the best of intentions, Quality Departments can make the mistake of turning EFQM assessment into a bureaucratic instrument instead of making it a creative and motivating tool.

The scoring of each criterion and sub-criterion is done by using questionnaires or forms (for more detail, visit national or international pages of EFQM) and applying the PDCA system, or RADAR logic, explained above.

Following the evaluation guidelines, the self-evaluation committee and later the external evaluator, if requested, awards points within the maximum of each sub-criterion, based on the detected evidence.

We reiterate that the **essence of the model is not the numerical scores but its usefulness** to indicate, for each of the nine pillars, to what extent an excellent management, or on the contrary, a very poor management is being performed.

The organization is not to serve the model, but the model to serve and guide the organization improvement. The great challenge for any evaluator is not scoring, something he should do, but, above all, validate and suggest areas for improvement.

During the scoring process the assessment of the different criteria **should keep certain internal consistency**. Thus, it would be illogical to assign a high score to Staff Management and a low score to Staff Satisfaction, because if a good staff management is carried out this would have a positive impact on the staff satisfaction.

Equally, it would be hardly reasonable to attribute a high score to Business Results and a low score to Processes and Resources Management, given the fact that the good results, except in very fortunate circumstances, are dependent on having the processes adequately updated and a good management of all resources.

In any case, those who wish to have a thorough understanding about the EFQM methodology are advised to study the specific publications or contact the European Foundation for Quality Management or the respective national, public or private organizations, accredited in the model.

17 CONCLUSIONS

Modern world is a changing reality that affects, to a greater or lesser extent, all countries in the world. The global scenario is varying very quickly. New information technologies, especially the Internet, the globalization of world markets and the growing relations between countries are setting a very different context to the one our parents knew.

Directors or managers today, both from the private and public sectors, are facing, more than ever, the challenge to manage their organizations, and therefore their human and material resources, successfully.

This involves refining many concepts of leadership that are still in force, and introducing revolutionary changes in the management model. Autocratic leadership will be forced, in a world of increasing complexity, to seek for the loyal contributions of its employees. This will require the managers to change their traditional attitude and sincerely become open to their employees participation.

Not even charismatic managers will remain as managers if they do not learn to treat their subordinates as adults. That again reiterates the need to set up more intensive participation systems. Excellence contains a coherent set of instructions and practices that ensures success in the management of organizations and prepares managers to respond to unforeseen adverse circumstances.

In a seminar organized at the Complutense University of Madrid in 1999 on *"Emerging trends in human resources management"* with the participation of the heads of major Spanish banks, companies specialized in staff management and Business Schools, it was noted, as a general conclusion, **that the main challenges** to human resources management at that time were:
- Knowledge management
- Human potential management
- Performance management
- Organizational Flexibility
- Optimization of Staff
- Participative leadership style

Those conclusions are still in force. Given the fact that the human factor is essential in any modern organization, Excellent HR management appears as a *sine qua non* for a good leadership.

Excellence offers **specific responses to all these challenges** that HR management faces:

1. Excellence emphasizes the importance of the Management of the **Employee's Knowledge.**

One of the cornerstones of Excellence is to enable the organization to benefit from all the potential for innovation that employees have with respect to the processes and products. Unfortunately, this potential is often squandered. Employees' ideas and suggestions are frequently ignored. As a result, they become reluctant to express new points of view.

The involvement of employees and especially their work in the Quality Circles is a suitable tool for managing the staff knowledge related to the improvement of production processes and product design.

2. Excellence feels responsible for the **Management of Employees' Potential**. Excellence proposes a leadership that is capable of raising the skills of the employees and promoting the development of their talents to their maximum contribution.

Do not forget that one of the most important factors for staff motivation is to provide them with opportunities to develop their talents and career.

3. Excellence promotes the **Performance Management** of employees and production units.

Excellence is **not just a mere declaration** of intentions and commitments by management and employees.

The figures, results and production rates are key specific information to help assess whether the activity of the organization is adequate or not. Therefore, they are indicators that help to decide whether to continue in the same way, in the same field or to do a radical change of direction.

The best way to obtain real data, not fictitious or masked, is to create an atmosphere of sincerity and loyalty among internal clients (the employees) and management.

Excellence proposes the **recognition** of the qualities and achievements of employees, and **avoids the obsession about finding who to blame** in order to punish them for their errors. This constructive attitude creates one of the best environments for an efficient Management performance.

4. Excellence facilitates **Flexibility of the Organization** because it prioritizes the mission achievement and besides, it pays close attention to the changing environment.

By observing changes in similar organizations and promoting the ongoing review of processes, Excellence leads to a rational and dynamic organizational adaptation to technological innovations and to the demands that come from changes in the processes.

5. Excellence facilitates **Staff Optimization.** The pledge of allegiance, reciprocal between managers and employees, promotes stability in the recruitment and reduces resistance to redeploying and moving the staff around.

6. Excellence stimulates the **Participative Leadership style** by emphasizing that without mobilizing the synergies and complementarities that exist within the organization, it will be difficult to achieve success.

The proper functioning of Quality Circles requires a clear commitment to participative management. In turn, the constructive proposals of Quality Circles intensify and reinforce the climate of participation.

7. **In addition to all the aforementioned aspects,** Excellence emphasizes the **Importance of the Mission**, which is the 'raison d'être' of the organization. This is achieved by **focusing on the Client,** who is the final and main receiver of the products that are the result of the Mission of the organization.

Excellence does so through **two main actions:**

A. It considers Client Satisfaction as a basic result indicator, because satisfaction has a great impact on the image of the organization and on the stability of the results.

If the customer becomes loyal to the company, the products will have a better sale. A stable clientele is a guarantee of future results for the company.

B. It consults the Cliente and analyses their opinions. It is not enough to wait for the clients to come and tell us that "*something is happening*". It is necessary to go after them actively and collect their opinions.

They are a very low-cost source of information (most of the clients' opinions are obtained for free) that can bring interesting suggestions.

Moreover, consulting the clients has the positive effect of linking them to the organization and this can be a channel of great importance when it comes to receiving suggestions about the creation of new products.

Besides, client's complaints or opinions facilitate the control of the efficiency of the production and delivery processes.

Summing up: Excellence is an effective and efficient management philosophy and technique.

It offers a **rational** and **holistic** approach that clarifies how to lead organizations to **success** and, why not, to a better world.

18 BIBLIOGRAPHY

English

Aguayo, Rafael *"Dr. Deming: The American Who Taught the Japanese about Quality"* (1991)

Crosby, Philip B. *"Quality Is Free"* (1979)

Crosby, Philip B. *"Quality Is Still Free: Making Quality Certain in Uncertain Times"* (1995)

Ishikawa, Kaoru *"What is Total Quality Control? The Japanese Way"* Prentice Hall (1985)

Juran, Joseph M. Juran and D. A. Blanton Godfrey *"Managerial Breakthrough: The Classic Book on Improving Management Performance"* (1995)

Juran, Joseph and Godfrey, A. Blanton *"Juran's Quality Handbook"* (1998)

Parasuraman *"Delivering Quality Service: Balancing Customer Perceptions and Expectations"* (New York: Free Press, 1990)

Peters y Waterman *"In Search of Excellence: Lessons from America's Best-Run Companies"*

Peters, Tom *"Thriving on Chaos: Handbook for a Management Revolution"* 1991

Peters, Tom *"The Pursuit of Wow! Every Person's Guide to Topsy-Turvy Times"* 1994

Rosander, AC *"Deming's 14 Points Applied to Services (Quality and Reliability)"* 1991

Semler, Ricardo. *"Maverick: The Success Story Behind the World's Most Unusual Workplace"* 1995

Spanish

Aguayo, Rafael *"El Método Deming"* Ed. Vergara Buenos Aires 1.993

Arriortúa, J.A *"López de Arriortúa según él"* Ed.Tikal 1994 Madrid

Arriortúa, J.A *"Tú puedes"* Ed.Lid 2010. 1.997 Madrid

Bueno, Eduardo *"La dirección eficiente"* Ed. Pirámide Madrid 1993

Chuen Tao, Luis Yu *"El Control de Calidad en la Empresa"* Ed.Deusto 1.990 Bilbao

Crosby, Philip B. *"Hablemos de calidad"* Ed. McGraw Hill. Madrid 1993

Deming, William *"Calidad, productividad y competitividad. La salida de la crisis"* Ed. Díaz-Santos. Madrid. 1989

Drucker, Peter *"Administración para el Futuro"* Ed. Parramon Barcelona 1.993

Grieco, Peter *"World Class. Excelencia empresarial"* Ed. Deusto, Bilbao. 1997

Hodgson y Crainer. *"Los hábitos de los grandes directivos"* Ed. Folio Barcelona 1994

Hörnell, Erik *"La competititividad a través de la productividad"* Ed. Folio. Barcelona 1.994

Ishikawa, Kaoru *"¿Qué es el Control Total de Calidad?"* Ed. Parramón 1994. Barcelona

Juran y Gryna. *"Manual de control de calidad"* Ed McGraw Hill, Madrid. 1993

Juran *"La planificación para la calidad"* Ed. Diaz Santos, Madrid.1990

Munro Faure, Lesley *"La Calidad Total en acción"* Ed.Folio 1994 Barcelona

Perez Gutiérrez, Marcial *"Como mejorar los métodos de trabajo"* Ed.Deusto 1.989 Bilbao

Peters, Tom *"En busca del Boom"* Ed. Deusto Bilbao 1.995

Peters y Waterman *"En busca de la Excelencia"* Ed. Folio 1.986

Peters y Austin *"Pasión por la excelencia"* 1992. Ed.Folio. Barcelona.

Peters, Tom *"Reinventando la excelencia"* Ediciones B Barcelona 1.993

Rosander, AC *"La búsqueda de la calidad en los servicios"* Ed. Diaz Santos. Madrid. 1992

Semler, Ricardo. *"Radical. El éxito de una empresa sorprendente"* Ed.Plaza Janés 1.993 Barcelona

Whitehill, Arthur *"Japanese Management"* (Ed.Routledge. Londres.)

Wooldridge, Adrian *"La hora de los gurúes"* Alianza Editorial. Madrid 1.998

www.ingramcontent.com/pod-product-compliance
Lightning Source LLC
Chambersburg PA
CBHW071756200526
45167CB00017B/80

Employers are responsible for providing a safe and healthy workplace for their employees. OSHA's role is to promote the safety and health of America's working men and women by setting and enforcing standards; providing training, outreach and education; establishing partnerships; and encouraging continual improvement in workplace safety and health.

This informational booklet provides a general overview of a particular topic related to OSHA standards. It does not alter or determine compliance responsibilities in OSHA standards or the *Occupational Safety and Health Act of 1970*. Because interpretations and enforcement policy may change over time, you should consult current OSHA administrative interpretations and decisions by the Occupational Safety and Health Review Commission and the courts for additional guidance on OSHA compliance requirements.

This publication is in the public domain and may be reproduced, fully or partially, without permission. Source credit is requested but not required.

This information is available to sensory impaired individuals upon request. Voice phone: (202) 693-1999; teletypewriter (TTY) number: (877) 889-5627.

Permit-Required Confined Spaces

U.S. Department of Labor

Occupational Safety and Health Administration

OSHA 3138-01R
2004

Contents

Introduction...3
Definitions...3
OSHA's Confined Space Standard...4
    Alternative to a full permit entry...4
Written Programs...6
Controlling Hazards...7
    Equipment for safe entry...7
    Detection of hazardous conditions...7
Informing Contract Employees...8
Entry Permits...8
    Cancelled entry permits...9
Worker Training...9
Assigned Duties...10
    Authorized entrant..10
    Attendant...10
    Entry supervisor...11
Emergencies...12
    Rescue service personnel...12
    Harnesses and retrieval lines...12
    MSDS...12
OSHA Assistance...13
    Safety and Health Program Management Guidelines...13
    State Programs...14
    Consultation Services...14
    Voluntary Protection Programs (VPP)...15
    Strategic Partnership Program...15
    Alliance Programs...15
    OSHA Training and Education...16
    Information Available Electronically...17
    OSHA Publications...17
    Contacting OSHA...18
OSHA Regional Offices...19

Introduction

Many workplaces contain spaces that are considered to be "confined" because their configurations hinder the activities of employees who must enter into, work in or exit from them. In many instances, employees who work in confined spaces also face increased risk of exposure to serious physical injury from hazards such as entrapment, engulfment and hazardous atmospheric conditions. Confinement itself may pose entrapment hazards and work in confined spaces may keep employees closer to hazards such as machinery components than they would be otherwise. For example, confinement, limited access and restricted airflow can result in hazardous conditions that would not normally arise in an open workplace.

The terms "permit-required confined space" and "permit space" refer to spaces that meet OSHA's definition of a "confined space" and contain health or safety hazards. For this reason, OSHA requires workers to have a permit to enter these spaces. Throughout this publication, the term "permit space" will be used to describe a "permit-required confined space."

Definitions

By definition, a **confined space**:
- Is large enough for an employee to enter fully and perform assigned work;
- Is not designed for continuous occupancy by the employee; and
- Has a limited or restricted means of entry or exit.

These spaces may include underground vaults, tanks, storage bins, pits and diked areas, vessels, silos and other similar areas.

By definition, a **permit-required confined space** has one or more of these characteristics:
- Contains or has the potential to contain a hazardous atmosphere;
- Contains a material with the potential to engulf someone who enters the space;
- Has an internal configuration that might cause an entrant to be trapped or asphyxiated by inwardly converging walls or by a

floor that slopes downward and tapers to a smaller cross section; and/or
- Contains any other recognized serious safety or health hazards.

OSHA's Confined Space Standard

OSHA's standard for confined spaces (29 CFR 1910.146) contains the requirements for practices and procedures to protect employ-ees in general industry from the hazards of entering permit spaces.

Employers in general industry must evaluate their workplaces to determine if spaces are permit spaces. (See flow chart, page 5.) If a workplace contains permit spaces, the employer must inform exposed employees of their existence, location and the hazards they pose. This can be done by posting danger signs such as "DANGER—PERMIT-REQUIRED CONFINED SPACE—AUTHORIZED ENTRANTS ONLY" or using an equally effective means.

If employees are not to enter and work in permit spaces, employers must take effective measures to prevent them from entering these spaces. If employees are expected to enter permit spaces, the employer must develop a written permit space program and make it available to employees or their representatives.

Alternative to a full permit entry

Under certain conditions described in the standard, the employer may use alternate procedures for worker entry into a permit space. For example, if an employer can demonstrate with monitoring and inspection data that the only hazard is an actual or potential hazardous atmosphere that can be made safe for entry using continuous forced air ventilation, the employer may be exempted from some requirements, such as permits and attendants. However, even in these circumstances, the employer must test the internal atmosphere of the space for oxygen content, flammable gases and vapors, and the potential for toxic air contaminants before any employee enters it. The employer must also provide continuous ventilation and verify that the required measurements are performed before entry.

Permit-Required Confined Space Decision Flow Chart

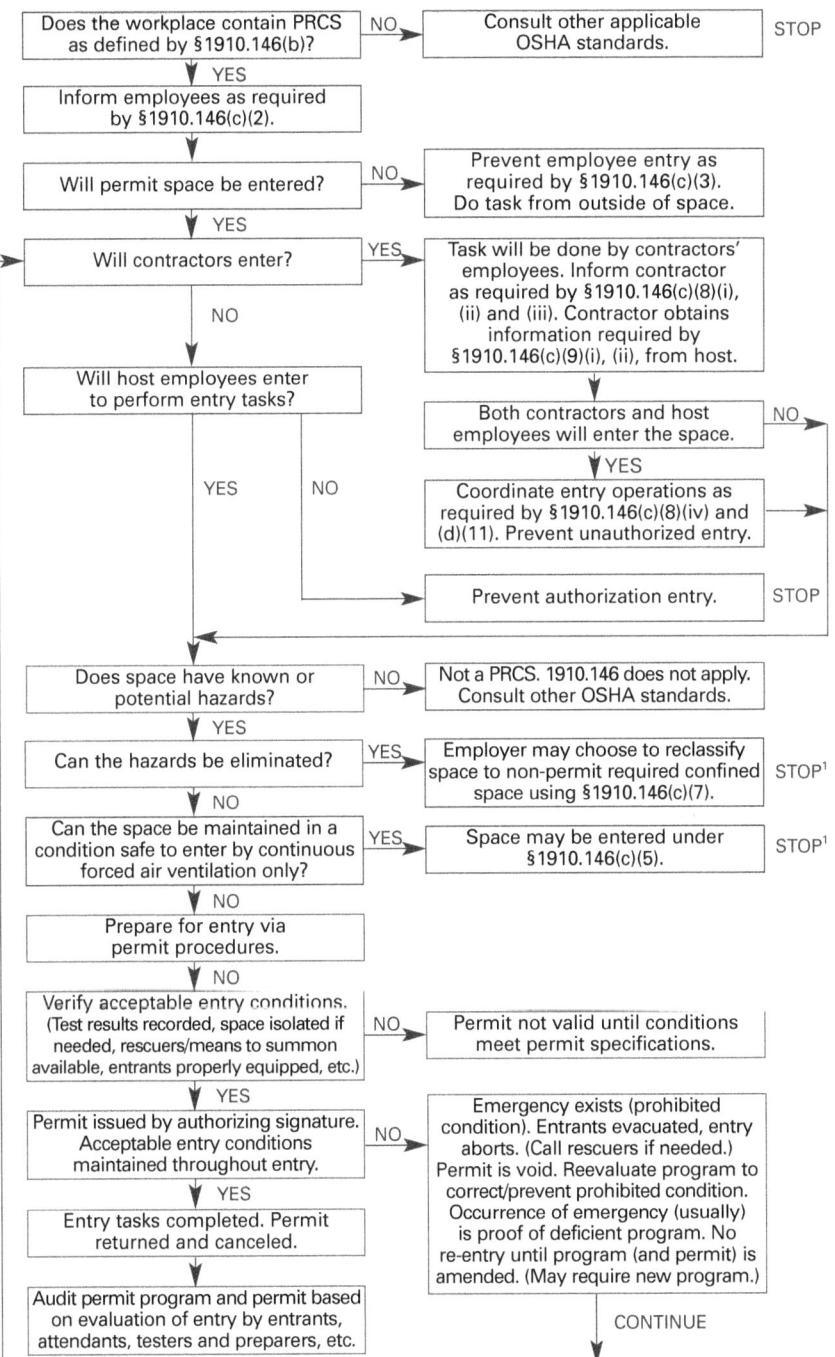

[1] Spaces may have to be evacuated and reevaluated if hazards arise during entry.

Source: 29 CFR 1910.146 Appendix A.

Written Programs

Any employer who allows employee entry into a permit space must develop and implement a written program for the space. Among other things, the OSHA standard requires the employer's written program to:

- Implement necessary measures to prevent unauthorized entry;
- Identify and evaluate permit space hazards before allowing employee entry;
- Test atmospheric conditions in the permit space before entry operations and monitor the space during entry;
- Perform appropriate testing for the following atmospheric hazards in this sequence: oxygen, combustible gases or vapors, and toxic gases or vapors;
- Establish and implement the means, procedures and practices to eliminate or control hazards necessary for safe permit space entry operations;
- Identify employee job duties;
- Provide and maintain, at no cost to the employee, personal protective equipment and any other equipment necessary for safe entry and require employees to use it;
- Ensure that at least one attendant is stationed outside the permit space for the duration of entry operations;
- Coordinate entry operations when employees of more than one employer are working in the permit space;
- Implement appropriate procedures for summoning rescue and emergency services, and preventing unauthorized personnel from attempting rescue;
- Establish, in writing, and implement a system for the preparation, issue, use and cancellation of entry permits;
- Review established entry operations annually and revise the permit space entry program as necessary; and
- Implement the procedures that any attendant who is required to monitor multiple spaces will follow during an emergency in one or more of those spaces.

Controlling Hazards

The employer's written program should establish the means, procedures and practices to eliminate or control hazards necessary for safe permit space entry operations. These may include:
- Specifying acceptable entry conditions;
- Isolating the permit space;
- Providing barriers;
- Verifying acceptable entry conditions; and
- Purging, making inert, flushing or ventilating the permit space.

Equipment for safe entry

In addition to personal protective equipment, other equipment that employees may require for safe entry into a permit space includes:
- Testing, monitoring, ventilating, communications and lighting equipment;
- Barriers and shields;
- Ladders; and
- Retrieval devices.

Detection of hazardous conditions

If hazardous conditions are detected during entry, employees must immediately leave the space. The employer must evaluate the space to determine the cause of the hazardous atmosphere and modify the program as necessary.

When entry to permit spaces is prohibited, the employer must take effective measures to prevent unauthorized entry. Non-permit confined spaces must be evaluated when changes occur in their use or configuration and, where appropriate, must be reclassified as permit spaces.

A space with no potential to have atmospheric hazards may be classified as a non-permit confined space only when all hazards are eliminated in accordance with the standard. If entry is required to eliminate hazards and obtain data, the employer must follow specific procedures in the standard.

Informing Contract Employees

Employers must inform any contractors whom they hire to enter permit spaces about:
- The permit spaces and permit space entry requirements;
- Any identified hazards;
- The employer's experience with the space, such as knowledge of hazardous conditions; and
- Precautions or procedures to be followed when in or near permit spaces.

When employees of more than one employer are conducting entry operations, the affected employers must coordinate entry operations to ensure that affected employees are appropriately protected from permit space hazards. The employer also must give contractors any other pertinent information regarding hazards and operations in permit spaces and be debriefed at the conclusion of entry operations.

Entry Permits

A permit, signed by the entry supervisor, must be posted at all entrances or otherwise made available to entrants before they enter a permit space. The permit must verify that pre-entry preparations outlined in the standard have been completed. The duration of entry permits must not exceed the time required to complete an assignment.

Entry permits must include:
- Name of permit space to be entered, authorized entrant(s), eligible attendants and individuals authorized to be entry supervisors;
- Test results;
- Tester's initials or signature;
- Name and signature of supervisor who authorizes entry;
- Purpose of entry and known space hazards;
- Measures to be taken to isolate permit spaces and to eliminate or control space hazards;

- Name and telephone numbers of rescue and emergency services and means to be used to contact them;
- Date and authorized duration of entry;
- Acceptable entry conditions;
- Communication procedures and equipment to maintain contact during entry;
- Additional permits, such as for hot work, that have been issued authorizing work in the permit space;
- Special equipment and procedures, including personal protective equipment and alarm systems; and
- Any other information needed to ensure employee safety.

Cancelled entry permits

The entry supervisor must cancel entry permits when an assignment is completed or when new conditions exist. New conditions must be noted on the canceled permit and used in revising the permit space program. The standard requires that the employer keep all canceled entry permits for at least one year.

Worker Training

Before the initial work assignment begins, the employer must provide proper training for all workers who are required to work in permit spaces. After the training, employers must ensure that the employees have acquired the understanding, knowledge and skills necessary to safely perform their duties. Additional training is required when:

- The job duties change;
- A change occurs in the permit space program or the permit space operation presents any new hazard; and
- An employee's job performance shows deficiencies.

In addition to this training, rescue team members also require training in CPR and first aid. Employers must certify that this training has been provided.

After completion of training, the employer must keep a record of employee training and make it available for inspection by employees

and their authorized representatives. The record must include the employee's name, the trainer's signature or initials and dates of the training.

Assigned Duties

Authorized entrant

Authorized entrants are required to:

- Know space hazards, including information on the means of exposure such as inhalation or dermal absorption, signs of symptoms and consequences of the exposure;
- Use appropriate personal protective equipment properly;
- Maintain communication with attendants as necessary to enable them to monitor the entrant's status and alert the entrant to evacuate when necessary;
- Exit from the permit space as soon as possible when:
  - Ordered by the authorized person;
  - He or she recognizes the warning signs or symptoms of exposure;
  - A prohibited condition exists; or
  - An automatic alarm is activated.
- Alert the attendant when a prohibited condition exists or when warning signs or symptoms of exposure exist.

Attendant

The attendant is required to:

- Remain outside the permit space during entry operations unless relieved by another authorized attendant;
- Perform non-entry rescues when specified by the employer's rescue procedure;
- Know existing and potential hazards, including information on the mode of exposure, signs or symptoms, consequences and physiological effects;

- Maintain communication with and keep an accurate account of those workers entering the permit space;
- Order evacuation of the permit space when:
  - A prohibited condition exists;
  - A worker shows signs of physiological effects of hazard exposure;
  - An emergency outside the confined space exists; and
  - The attendant cannot effectively and safely perform required duties.
- Summon rescue and other services during an emergency;
- Ensure that unauthorized people stay away from permit spaces or exit immediately if they have entered the permit space;
- Inform authorized entrants and the entry supervisor if any unauthorized person enters the permit space; and
- Perform no other duties that interfere with the attendant's primary duties.

Entry supervisor

Entry supervisors are required to:
- Know space hazards including information on the mode of exposure, signs or symptoms and consequences;
- Verify emergency plans and specified entry conditions such as permits, tests, procedures and equipment before allowing entry;
- Terminate entry and cancel permits when entry operations are completed or if a new condition exists;
- Verify that rescue services are available and that the means for summoning them are operable;
- Take appropriate measures to remove unauthorized entrants; and
- Ensure that entry operations remain consistent with the entry permit and that acceptable entry conditions are maintained.

Emergencies

Rescue service personnel

The standard requires employers to ensure that responders are capable of responding to an emergency in a timely manner. Employers must provide rescue service personnel with personal protective and rescue equipment, including respirators, and training in how to use it. Rescue service personnel also must receive the authorized entrants training and be trained to perform assigned rescue duties.

The standard also requires that all rescuers be trained in first aid and CPR. At a minimum, one rescue team member must be currently certified in first aid and CPR. Employers must ensure that practice rescue exercises are performed yearly and that rescue services are provided access to permit spaces so they can practice rescue operations. Rescuers also must be informed of the hazards of the permit space.

Harnesses and retrieval lines

Authorized entrants who enter a permit space must wear a chest or full body harness with a retrieval line attached to the center of their backs near shoulder level or above their heads. Wristlets may be used if the employer can demonstrate that the use of a chest or full body harness is not feasible or creates a greater hazard.

Also, the employer must ensure that the other end of the retrieval line is attached to a mechanical device or a fixed point outside the permit space. A mechanical device must be available to retrieve someone from vertical type permit spaces more than five feet (1.524 meters) deep.

MSDS

If an injured entrant is exposed to a substance for which a Material Safety Data Sheet (MSDS) or other similar written information is required to be kept at the worksite, that MSDS or other written information must be made available to the medical facility personnel treating the exposed entrant.

OSHA Assistance

OSHA can provide extensive help through a variety of programs, including technical assistance about effective safety and health programs, state plans, workplace consultations, voluntary protection programs, strategic partnerships, training and education, and more. An overall commitment to workplace safety and health can add value to your business, to your workplace, and to your life.

Safety and Health Program Management Guidelines

Effective management of employee safety and health protection is a decisive factor in reducing the extent and severity of work-related injuries and illnesses and their related costs. In fact, an effective safety and health program forms the basis of good employee protection and can save time and money and increase productivity and reduce employee injuries, illnesses, and related workers' compensation costs.

To assist employers and employees in developing effective safety and health programs, OSHA published recommended Safety and Health Program Management Guidelines (54 Federal Register (16): 3904-3916, January 26, 1989). These voluntary guidelines can be applied to all places of employment covered by OSHA.

The guidelines identify four general elements critical to the development of a successful safety and health management system:

- Management leadership and employee involvement,
- Worksite analysis,
- Hazard prevention and control, and
- Safety and health training.

The guidelines recommend specific actions, under each of these general elements, to achieve an effective safety and health program. The *Federal Register* notice is available online at www.osha.gov.

State Programs

The *Occupational Safety and Health Act of 1970* (OSH Act) encourages states to develop and operate their own job safety and health plans. OSHA approves and monitors these plans. Twenty-four states, Puerto Rico and the Virgin Islands currently operate approved state plans: 22 cover both private and public (state and local government) employment; Connecticut, New Jersey, New York and the Virgin Islands cover the public sector only. States and territories with their own OSHA-approved occupational safety and health plans must adopt standards identical to, or at least as effective as, the Federal OSHA standards.

Consultation Services

Consultation assistance is available on request to employers who want help in establishing and maintaining a safe and healthful workplace. Largely funded by OSHA, the service is provided at no cost to the employer. Primarily developed for smaller employers with more hazardous operations, the consultation service is delivered by state governments employing professional safety and health consultants. Comprehensive assistance includes an appraisal of all mechanical systems, work practices, and occupational safety and health hazards of the workplace and all aspects of the employer's present job safety and health program. In addition, the service offers assistance to employers in developing and implementing an effective safety and health program. No penalties are proposed or citations issued for hazards identified by the consultant. OSHA provides consultation assistance to the employer with the assurance that his or her name and firm and any information about the workplace will not be routinely reported to OSHA enforcement staff.

Under the consultation program, certain exemplary employers may request participation in OSHA's Safety and Health Achievement Recognition Program (SHARP). Eligibility for participation in SHARP includes receiving a comprehensive consultation visit, demonstrating exemplary achievements in workplace safety and health by abating all identified hazards, and developing an excellent safety and health program.

Employers accepted into SHARP may receive an exemption from programmed inspections (not complaint or accident investigation inspections) for a period of 1 year. For more information concerning consultation assistance, see OSHA's website at www.osha.gov.

Voluntary Protection Programs (VPP)

Voluntary Protection Programs and on-site consultation services, when coupled with an effective enforcement program, expand employee protection to help meet the goals of the OSH Act. The VPPs motivate others to achieve excellent safety and health results in the same outstanding way as they establish a cooperative relationship between employers, employees, and OSHA.

For additional information on VPP and how to apply, contact the OSHA regional offices listed at the end of this publication.

Strategic Partnership Program

OSHA's Strategic Partnership Program, the newest member of OSHA's cooperative programs, helps encourage, assist, and recognize the efforts of partners to eliminate serious workplace hazards and achieve a high level of employee safety and health. Whereas OSHA's Consultation Program and VPP entail one-on-one relationships between OSHA and individual worksites, most strategic partnerships seek to have a broader impact by building cooperative relationships with groups of employers and employees. These partnerships are voluntary, cooperative relationships between OSHA, employers, employee representatives, and others (e.g., trade unions, trade and professional associations, universities, and other government agencies).

For more information on this and other cooperative programs, contact your nearest OSHA office, or visit OSHA's website at www.osha.gov.

Alliance Program

Through the Alliance Program, OSHA works with groups committed to safety and health, including businesses, trade or professional organizations, unions and educational institutions, to leverage resources and expertise to develop compliance assistance tools and resources and share information with employers and employees to help prevent injuries, illnesses and fatalities in the workplace.

Alliance Program agreements have been established with a wide variety of industries including meat, apparel, poultry, steel, plastics, maritime, printing, chemical, construction, paper and telecommunications. These agreements are addressing many safety and health hazards and at-risk audiences; including silica, fall protection, amputations, immigrant workers, youth and small businesses. By meeting the goals of the Alliance Program agreements (training and education, outreach and communication, and promoting the national dialogue on workplace safety and health), OSHA and the Alliance Program participants are developing and disseminating compliance assistance information and resources for employers and employees such as electronic assistance tools, fact sheets, toolbox talks, and training programs.

OSHA Training and Education

OSHA area offices offer a variety of information services, such as compliance assistance, technical advice, publications, audiovisual aids and speakers for special engagements. OSHA's Training Institute in Arlington Heights, IL, provides basic and advanced courses in safety and health for Federal and state compliance officers, state consultants, Federal agency personnel, and private sector employers, employees, and their representatives.

The OSHA Training Institute also has established OSHA Training Institute Education Centers to address the increased demand for its courses from the private sector and from other federal agencies. These centers are nonprofit colleges, universities, and other organizations that have been selected after a competition for participation in the program.

OSHA also provides funds to nonprofit organizations, through grants, to conduct workplace training and education in subjects where OSHA believes there is a lack of workplace training. Grants are awarded annually. Grant recipients are expected to contribute 20 percent of the total grant cost.

For more information on grants, training, and education, contact the OSHA Training Institute, Directorate of Training and Education, 2020 South Arlington Road, Arlington Heights, IL 60005, (847) 297-4810, or see *Outreach* on OSHA's website at www.osha.gov. For further information on any OSHA program, contact your nearest OSHA regional office listed at the end of this publication.

Information Available Electronically

OSHA has a variety of materials and tools available on its website at www.osha.gov. These include electronic compliance assistance tools, such as Safety and Health Topics, eTools, Expert Advisors; regulations, directives and publications; videos and other information for employers and employees. OSHA's software programs and compliance assistance tools walk you through challenging safety and health issues and common problems to find the best solutions for your workplace.

A wide variety of OSHA materials, including standards, interpretations, directives and more can be purchased on CD-ROM from the U.S. Government Printing Office, Superintendent of Documents, toll-free phone (866) 512-1800.

OSHA Publications

OSHA has an extensive publications program. For a listing of free or sales items, visit OSHA's website at www.osha.gov or contact the OSHA Publications Office, U.S. Department of Labor, 200 Constitution Avenue, NW, N-3101, Washington, DC 20210: Telephone (202) 693-1888 or fax to (202) 693-2498.

Contacting OSHA

To report an emergency, file a complaint, or seek OSHA advice, assistance, or products, call (800) 321-OSHA or contact your nearest OSHA Regional or Area office listed at the end of this publication. The teletypewriter (TTY) number is (877) 889-5627.

Written correspondence can be mailed to the nearest OSHA Regional or Area Office listed at the end of this publication or to OSHA's national office at: U.S. Department of Labor, Occupational Safety and Health Administration, 200 Constitution Avenue, N.W., Washington, DC 20210.

By visiting OSHA's website at www.osha.gov, you can also:
- file a complaint online,
- submit general inquiries about workplace safety and health electronically, and
- find more information about OSHA and occupational safety and health.

OSHA Regional Offices

Region I
(CT,* ME, MA, NH, RI, VT*)
JFK Federal Building, Room E340
Boston, MA 02203
(617) 565-9860

Region II
(NJ,* NY,* PR,* VI*)
201 Varick Street, Room 670
New York, NY 10014
(212) 337-2378

Region III
(DE, DC, MD,* PA, VA,* WV)
The Curtis Center
170 S. Independence Mall West
Suite 740 West
Philadelphia, PA 19106-3309
(215) 861-4900

Region IV
(AL, FL, GA, KY,* MS, NC,* SC,* TN*)
61 Forsyth Street, SW, Room 6T50
Atlanta, GA 30303
(404) 562-2300

Region V
(IL, IN,* MI,* MN,* OH, WI)
230 South Dearborn Street
Room 3244
Chicago, IL 60604
(312) 353-2220

Region VI
(AR, LA, NM,* OK, TX)
525 Griffin Street, Room 602
Dallas, TX 75202
(972) 850-4145

Region VII
(IA,* KS, MO, NE)
Two Pershing Square
2300 Main Street, Suite 1010
Kansas City, MO 64108-2416
(816) 283-8745

Region VIII
(CO, MT, ND, SD, UT,* WY*)
1999 Broadway, Suite 1690
PO Box 46550
Denver, CO 80202-5716
(720) 264-6550

Region IX
(AZ,* CA,* HI,* NV,* and
American Samoa, Guam and
the Northern Mariana Islands)
90 7th Street, Suite 18-100
San Francisco, CA 94103
(415) 625-2547

Region X
(AK,* ID, OR,* WA*)
1111 Third Avenue, Suite 715
Seattle, WA 98101-3212
(206) 553-5930

* These states and territories operate their own OSHA-approved job safety and health programs and cover state and local government employees as well as private sector employees. The Connecticut, New Jersey, New York and Virgin Islands plans cover public employees only. States with approved programs must have standards that are identical to, or at least as effective as, the Federal OSHA standards.

Note: To get contact information for OSHA Area Offices, OSHA-approved State Plans and OSHA Consultation Projects, please visit us online at www.osha.gov or call us at 1-800-321-0SHA.